LEADING THE THIRD WORKFORCE

Integrating AI Into Your Team Without Losing the Human Edge

Jeff Lupinacci

Jasper House Press

Printed in the United States.

Jasper House Press | website www.jasperhousepress.com

Cover Design: Jennifer Welch

Interior Design: Jennifer Welch

Cataloging-in-publication Data is on file with the Library of Congress.

ISBN: 979-8-9905478-3-4

Praise for *The Talent Advantage*

"*The Talent Advantage* is a strategic playbook highlighting talent's critical role in achieving your mission. Jeff is the Top Gun of hiring, talent, and human resources. This book is a must-read for leaders committed to victory!"

—Ed Rush, ***Former Top Gun Fighter Pilot and #1 Best Selling Author***

"When I became CEO of our company five years ago, we had been stuck in a season of plateaued growth and stagnation. Through years of hard work, driven by investment in our talent and ensuring we had the right people on the bus and in the right seats, we have managed to build momentum and have record years of growth. I only wish I had *The Talent Advantage* as by guide book for the long trek we have been though. This excellent book provides a clear, practical and adaptable blueprint to accelerate growth and momentum no matter what situation you find your business in. Borrowing from the engaging business fable that serves as the foundation of *The Talent Advantage*, Jeff Lupinacci is your Talent Guide with a step-by-step to differentiate your business in the competitive marketplace and outpace your competitors in accelerating long-term success and employee recruitment, engagement, and retention. Save yourself years of frustration and struggle by buying this book now to guide your talent transformation."

—Tim Lupinacci, ***CEO Baker Donelson***

"*The Talent Advantage* weaves a wonderful tapestry of human resource threads to share the importance of how talent drives and even accelerates growth. It's relevant, timely, and adaptable."
—Frederick "Fritz" Maier, ***former CHRO Fanatics***

"Jeff did an incredible job humanizing the story about a CEO learning to fuel company growth with the best talent. The narrative is fast-paced and engaging, making it a fun read. The characters are well-developed and relatable, allowing readers to connect with their own experiences. This is a must read for any people leader."
—Steve Kimball, ***Talent Executive***

"*The Talent Advantage* is a must read for HR professionals seeking practical guidance on managing talent: having the right people with the right skills in the right positions to contribute to the growth, success and impact of the organization. "
— Clarissa Mitchell, ***Talent Executive***

"Finally, relatable fiction for HR Professionals to understand and apply to their roles as we face the ever-changing work environment and the war for talent head on. *The Talent Advantage* is a masterful guide for any leader looking to harness the full potential of their workforce and turn their talent into the competitive advantage for their organization. It recognizes from the first story the impact that people have on the profitability and future success of an organization. Jeff's keen insights and practical strategies for distilling complex human resources principles into actionable steps, which drive real results, is brilliant. As a Senior HR Executive, I

finally have a kindred spirit. Insightful, strategic, and real."
—D'Mar Philips, ***Senior HR Executive***

"*The Talent Advantage* is a must-read for anyone interested in business and leadership."
—Joy D'Amore, ***HR Executive***

"*The Talent Advantage* is a guidebook for business leaders in all industries interested in improving results. Without people, there is no company, just like without sports players, there is no team. This book offers an easily digestible way to evaluate leadership and employee talent, and use the strengths of that combined talent to accelerate your business. Buy a copy for yourself and your team."
— Deborah Hill, ***HR Executive***

To my grandchildren. You are the future workforce that inspires me to see the current work environment and culture change for the better.

TABLE OF CONTENTS

Introduction

More than twenty-five years ago, I was part of the early push toward what we then called e-business. I was working at Intel when the company was aggressively becoming a fully digital enterprise. The goal of removing manual work was straightforward, even if the implications for the work or the employees were not. We worked to automate as much of the process as possible and to allow transactions to move freely from beginning to end without interruption.

In that environment, I was asked to focus on a strategic question: What happens when we automate a complete process? What happens when no human has to touch the work? What risks were involved, what issues do we need to be on the lookout for, and how do we ensure we capture the benefits while remaining in control?

That question led to the development of a transaction governance strategy. At its core, it was an attempt to understand how data moves through a business and where risk begins to show up when that movement is no longer visible to the people responsible for it. We were dealing with processes like procure-to-pay, where a single input, something as simple as a price, could move through multiple steps and trigger downstream actions without anyone stopping to validate it. Once the transaction was initiated, the system would proceed even if the underlying data was incorrect.

At the time, the technology's capability was in its infancy and could not completely remove people from the process. There were still natural touch points where someone would need to review, question, or correct the errors. Those activities acted as a control point, whether we labeled them that way or not. While the risk was there, it was still somewhat contained, and we decided to put the strategy on a shelf.

When I first saw what AI could do, I realized it was the missing piece to realizing a 100% e-business company. The change in real capability, namely AI, filled in those gaps that acted as control points. Now the system could do all of the work, and in many cases, a human never has to look at it. It's at this point that I realized the same question asked two decades ago still apply.

What happens when no one is really looking at the work as it moves through the process? What I hadn't anticipated was how AI would extend beyond automating a manual process. I didn't realize AI would determine what to do with a transaction, make decisions, and take on the work humans have done for decades. Again, in that moment, I realized we had a new workforce to deal with, not just employees or contractors. AI would now be a third part of the workforce, capable of taking on jobs that historically were reserved for humans. And that, this Third Workforce, would change how companies viewed people and talent from here on out–for better or worse.

Though some components have evolved, the strategy I learned and implemented twenty-five years ago still holds. In our attempt to run into the unknown world of AI, we forgot the lessons of yesterday, and many companies are now facing the reality that implementing AI is not like implementing an ERP or CRM. Treating it simply as a technical solution without understanding how the human owner fits in is short-sighted and creates gaps in processes, governance, and people's capabilities.

This book is an attempt to address that gap, provide practical ways to solve the issues, and establish a structured process for the future. My goal is to help leaders understand how to incorporate the solutions in ways that strengthen the enterprise as a whole. I chose to keep this story within the world of *The Talent Advantage* for a reason. Most leaders are not dealing with these seismic changes in isolation. They are working through them within existing teams, organizational structures, and employee relationships. The same people who built the current system are now being asked to transform it.

If I can be honest with you, no one needed another book telling people how to manage AI in theory. It also doesn't help that many of the AI gurus are all academic or theoretical. Writing a book based on thirty years of working with people and technology, and living through similar world-changing technology, allowed me to share what I learned in a real-world setting.

The world of former CEO Richard Curtis is a way to bring practical solutions into a setting most of you will understand. Five years have passed, and a lot has changed in the life of the company. The new CEO decided to go all-in on AI, and by the time the issues surfaced, the Board realized it needed to take drastic steps to save the company. They will learn how to reframe AI in the workplace, engage their workforce to rebuild trust, and develop a structure to better govern AI.

I hope you enjoy and learn practical tools as you journey with Richard and his team through these pages.

Gratefully,
Jeff Lupinacci

Prologue
A System Turned

Marcus slammed his car door harder than he intended, and his cappuccino decided to slide off the top of the car, where he had placed it before reaching into the car to grab his briefcase. The lid bounced once on the ground before getting lost under his vehicle. A ribbon of coffee splashed down his pant leg and soaked directly into his right shoe.

"Perfect. Just perfect," Marcus muttered to no one in particular as he looked up to the sky.

He stared at the mess in slow disbelief, patting uselessly at the stain with a napkin that disintegrated halfway through the job. Migraines had been hitting him for weeks, each one sharper than the last, and his morning ritual—a cappuccino from the café across town—was supposed to give him at least a little clarity before the storm of the day hit.

No such luck today. But that wasn't new.

Inside the building, his receptionist looked up, noticing the stain on his wet pant leg as he entered the lobby. She opened her mouth to offer help but wisely closed it again. Marcus didn't slow down. He kept a backup suit in his office for emergencies like this. He had never thought to keep extra socks, an oversight in his planning that he now deeply regretted.

He had just sat at his desk and began reading an email when his office door opened suddenly. Dane and Nate walked in, both wearing expressions that Marcus instantly knew he would not enjoy this conversation.

Dane shut the door behind them. "Marcus, I'll get straight to it," he said. "We've decided to make a leadership change."

Marcus blinked, not expecting this turn of events. "A leadership change?"

"You're out," Nate said, stepping forward. "We're bringing in a new CEO. We'll need you to clear out your desk." He eyed the drying coffee stains on Marcus's shirt with obvious disdain.

Marcus leaned back in his chair, the news landing like a blow to the chest. "I see," he said, taking a measured breath before asking, "May I ask: why now?"

Dane spoke up, "We've evaluated the trajectory, and we're not where we need to be. This business needs a reset, and it needs it immediately."

Marcus opened his mouth, maybe to argue, maybe to defend himself, but Dane was already sliding a manila envelope onto the desk. "A severance package is in your contract, which you are well aware of. You can take it home and call if you have any questions."

And just like that, forty-three seconds later, the meeting was over. The door stayed open behind them. Marcus stared at the envelope, feeling heat rise behind his eyes as anger, humiliation, and disbelief fought for space. He did not expect Richard to follow through with his comments from the week before. He knew he was in trouble, but he hoped to have more time. He understood this was life in private equity, but he never thought it would be his life.

A week. He had one week to change course, and Marcus convinced himself that the warning was just bluster. He still had time, he told himself. Time to turn the numbers around. Time to win them back. No one honestly expected a turnaround in a week... But in private equity, time was not one of the things leaders had. It was about the results, by you or the person after your dismissal. And this time, they weren't bluffing when they gave the deadline.

His assistant appeared in the doorway– his former assistant. "They asked me to pack up your things," she said gently. "I've been told I need to escort you out."

And that was it, two years of effort condensed into a walk down the hallway that felt longer than his entire career. The AC kicked on as he stood up, and a cool blast of air hit his suit, giving him chills as he walked out the door.

The drive home was a blur of half-remembered traffic lights and stop signs. His thoughts played back the past two years of work at the company. He believed he could outsmart the economic downturn. He was certain he could "lean out" the organization, saving costs and driving productivity. For a while, it appeared it might even work.

He cut overtime and consolidated roles. He launched dashboards that looked good in board decks, even if no one used them. He was proud to say that they had implemented AI tools across the entire business. They moved fast and forced the teams to adopt them. They began cutting headcount as soon as the new tools were implemented. The ROI suggested that the AI tools would produce ten times as much work as an employee. He didn't care that employees hated AI. He had driven enough transformations to know that employees never liked change. He didn't understand why the results didn't look like they thought they would.

However, as he thought about it more, the warning signs had been there all along; he just refused to see them. Marcus had told himself he needed time for everyone to get on board to leave for greener pastures–time he no longer had. Obviously, there was something he missed.

As memories continued to flood his mind, a recent encounter with a customer stung, given the day's events. The buyer decided to stop the meeting halfway through Marcus's presentation. "We don't recognize your company anymore," she had said. "And we're not convinced you are serious about doing business with us."

He had ignored that, too. He continued to work hard, picking up the slack and managing everything efficiently using his proven system. A system that had just turned on him. His migraine throbbed behind his temples.

Chapter One
The Fall

Marcus continued thinking about how he got here: the purgatory of transition. His mind drifted back years, to the start of the journey that shaped him into the leader he had become, wondering where he had gone wrong.

He remembered his old home nestled in a modest neighborhood in Syracuse. Like many in the community, his parents worked long hours in hopes of building a better life for him and his siblings. Though he never heard them complain, he remembered the muffled arguments behind closed doors and sighs when bills came due. The kids at school never quite accepted him because his stuff wasn't new enough, nice enough. Then, a string of memories surfaced of his parents encouraging him to work hard, to do better, to make more of himself; and he did; there wasn't a particular moment that stood out, but conversations, comments, watching his parent's silent struggle, and the realization that to make life what you want it, you had to work hard and take it for yourself was his main takeaway from childhood.

Marcus decided early in his life that he would not allow himself to get into the kind of situation his parents were in: happy but never having enough. He would not wait for retirement to enjoy life; instead, he decided — when was it, seventh grade, eighth grade? —to drive himself to ensure he always had enough. More than enough, if he was honest with himself.

Another memory surfaced. In school, he was quiet and usually kept to himself. Sitting in the back of the room, he observed mostly. When he did engage, his teachers noticed how well he grasped complex ideas. His parents didn't notice that he took AP classes, but his teachers did. He could still picture his AP Macroeconomics teacher, Mr. Burk, calling him up to the front of the class to congratulate him on his perfect score on not one, but two tests in a row. He beamed with pride, standing there before his jealous classmates. That was the moment Marcus learned how good it felt to be recognized, and how he loved the possibilities of economics. Marcus's desire to understand how business worked set him apart long before he realized it.

The long hours studying earned him a scholarship to NYU. He could still feel the shock he experienced when driving into the City, knowing it was going to be his home; suddenly, he felt he had entered a new world, one that was noisier and more competitive than he could have imagined.

It took him a few weeks to learn the rhythms of the city. Once he experienced the pace and energy, he found the rhythm. He felt alive, he thought with nostalgia. As in high school, his professors recognized his systematic thinking. He excelled in every class he took, and many professors took an immediate liking to him, if for no other reason than he was their top student. That professor of Quantitative Analysis actually used his project as an example for the other students. Who was it that said the professor was still using it in their class, years later? Doesn't matter now, he thought.

His professors made sure the big consulting firms paid attention, as well. He graduated at the top of his class, interviewed with three global firms, and received offers from all of them. Tony couldn't believe it, which felt good. "I've lived with you these last four years, we've taken the same classes, we're graduating with the same degree, but you actually know what you're doing–and have options post-grad. How the Hell did you pull that off, man?"

Looking back, he was grateful to have taken a consulting role first. The type of work exposed Marcus to all aspects of business: operations, finance, supply chains, and restructuring. He learned how companies function at their best and how they break down at their worst.

Through it all, he saw that the leaders who could lead companies through even the worst messes all had a certain kind of charisma that drew people to them, and he quickly learned to develop that confidence within himself. The charisma he nurtured forced all eyes to turn to him, even when he walked into a boardroom full of experienced executives. Those first few tries were awful! he thought, chuckling. Soon, he would figure out how to command attention in every meeting, even with his managers at the firm. He could also understand exactly where the numbers fell apart or explain the issues in a way that made people listen, allowing him to rise in the ranks. He learned how to build models that forecast cash flow, redesign operational workflows, and identify organizational problems long before they appeared in the financial statements.

Eventually, Marcus realized he wanted to lead the organization and own the results himself. He was tired of being the one to recommend the right answer. Instead, he wanted the authority to do things his way. So when a private equity partner approached him after twelve years in the field and asked if he'd take the lead of a struggling manufacturing company, Marcus didn't hesitate. It was the natural next step, Marcus thought. A chance to apply everything he'd learned, and to prove to himself that he could do it.

Stepping into his first CEO role was a whirlwind of long days and learning everything there was to know about the company. He began his tenure at the company with a clear mission to understand every detail of the financials, meet with every department head, and tour every plant. Once he had the lay of the land, he immediately started restructuring. He cut costs carefully, closed unprofitable lines, renegotiated contracts, and enforced discipline across the company- all standard stuff, but the CEO before hadn't thought of it; Marcus had. Within eighteen months, EBITDA increased. The valuation followed. When it was time to sell, everyone celebrated the turnaround and the pro forma value it created. Everyone made a fortune from his first stint as CEO. They celebrated him. They made a fortune because of him. Chris even nicknamed him the "Darling of the Principles."

He had delivered on his promise and proven something to

the investors, his team, and, perhaps most of all, to himself. He proved he could do it, and his system worked. That's what he couldn't understand now. Why, when did it stop working? For years, it worked.

The private equity firms kept calling after each successful exit. He still remembered each call. The excitement of a new opportunity. He made the next chapter of his career by moving from one struggling company to another, following a tried-and-true process he developed. With each new company, he would show up and assess all the systems and processes. Then he would lean out the costs, and push for improved productivity. He honed his system; yes, it was essentially the same one he created during his tenure at the first company, but the results spoke for themselves. He became known for what he could do, driving hard change, imposing discipline, simplifying operations, and increasing company multiples that made their owners a lot of money. Marcus benefited from those exits, as well. No one ever complained then.

He knew he worked at a relentless pace, and if he could do it, his people needed to be able to keep up. Since he didn't have time to handhold any whiners, many considered him cruel, though that was not entirely accurate. He retained a little of his compassion, but he was not a patient man. Karla, Joan, and their divorce lawyers could all testify to that. He prioritized speed and efficiency above all else. Investors admired him for his drive. It was clear that the PE world had changed him, but he was finally comfortable, living the life he had always dreamed of.

When he took the CEO position at this company, the largest he had ever led, it felt like the culmination of everything he had worked toward. It was a solid company with a tremendous growth trajectory, and it was a new situation for Marcus; an opportunity to leave a lasting mark and demonstrate that he could scale his formula to a larger, more complex organization, especially one that didn't need the turnaround. He arrived with a plan before he had even met half the executive team. There was nothing wrong with coming in prepared, but he remembered it rubbed some of the team, who had been there longer, the wrong way. Their problem, not mine, he thought, and he immediately started looking into replacing the executive employees he knew would create obstacles and delays.

His first call was to Emily. She had worked with him at

two previous companies. She was as disciplined as he was and understood his way of thinking. She even knew how to turn his ambitions into financial models and detailed plans. Together, on that call, they decided to bring in Brianne, a rising star in AI transformation, to lead the company into what Marcus believed was the next stage of operational excellence.

Marcus became infatuated with AI as the ideal tool to accelerate his turnarounds. It held the promise of faster decision-making, reduced costs, and the removal of flawed human judgment from the process. It was an opportunity to modernize faster than their competitors, drive bottom-line efficiencies, and bring their products to market faster than ever before.

So, of course, he went all in. And, maybe that was the beginning of the end. But, no, they did see progress.

He mandated the adoption of AI throughout the business. Everyone scrambled to implement the systems quickly, often before the teams were ready to use them, but he knew progress often necessitated a leap. People were naturally lazy and needed a push from time to time. Marcus believed that bold moves required bold timelines. Maybe he pushed the team to move faster than they were comfortable with and implement systems they didn't fully understand. For a time, at least, the numbers agreed with his approach. Costs decreased, driving a rapid rise in EBITDA. Investors were excited about the early momentum. Marcus felt validated and even energized by his success.

He didn't see the problems brewing under his nose. He was told team leaders began to feel overwhelmed and unsure how to use the newly implemented tools. Data quality issues led to incorrect results because no one was monitoring the AI process. He did remember overhearing two employees speaking in the break room one time. They didn't see him, but he heard a whisper that leadership was using technology to spy on them. How absurd, he thought. Why did he still remember that ridiculous comment?

He did see glimpses of eroding customer trust. Complaints began to rise, from customers and employees. When the market shifted and sales slowed down, Marcus still believed his strategy would hold. He thought the AI-driven cost cuts would provide him with some protection.

And yet, as he drove home, his reality hit him like a ton

of bricks. He always believed his superpower was seeing the best ways to cut costs and prepare a company for sale. However, guiding a company through genuine transformation required something different. But what?

Lost in his thoughts, another memory surfaced, one Marcus had brushed aside at the time.

It was late one evening, near the start of the AI rollout. The plant was mostly empty, the kind of quiet that settles over a building when the day's urgency finally fades away. Marcus and David walked out together, both heading to their cars. Marcus felt proud. The first wave of automation dashboards had just gone live, and the initial cost savings were finally starting to show up in the numbers.

As they reached their cars, David said, shaking his head, "It looks like I'm the last one standing from the old team. If I'm being honest, I didn't expect that. I figured you'd replace me with a bot by now."

Marcus laughed at David's humor. "Not to worry, you're safe," he said, clapping David on the shoulder. "Besides, the new tools will make your job easier. We are living in the future, and you get to be part of it."

David smiled. "Thank you. But I'm more worried about the employees as they're overwhelmed with the pace of change. Some teams refuse to use the tools while others think it's Big Brother watching, trying to see who's next."

Marcus waved a hand dismissively. "That always happens at first. Resistance is part of the curve. You know that. I've run this playbook several times already. They just need a little time to adjust. Those who don't will leave and we will be better off for it."

David didn't back down. He leaned against his truck and crossed his arms. "I understand. I've been part of a big change before, but this time it is different. My best guess is we're outpacing the employees' ability to absorb the change. I'm not sure the rollout is landing the way we think it is."

Marcus remembered he was eager to end the conversation. "Look, I appreciate the concern. Really. But I am right. I've run this play before, and the numbers are already turning in our favor. We just need to give it time. If you are that worried about the people, spend some time with them, but don't let their change resistance distract you from the growth objectives we have."

David nodded; there was no resolution, even though the conversation was over. "All right," he said. "Time will tell."

Marcus had gotten into his car that night feeling confident, knowing he was right. It didn't occur to him to wonder why David, a steady and level-headed leader, looked troubled as he drove away.

Marcus now realized he hadn't listened to David. He simply dismissed his concern because it didn't fit his story. He knew systems, and this was part of the process. His experience told him he was right, and he had seen every form of resistance. His pride led him to believe he didn't need another point of view. And yet, now that the unthinkable had happened, he couldn't shake that parking lot conversation. David had warned him that the people were not ready for the tools they were implementing.

"Had I really forgotten about the people?" Marcus said to himself as he turned into his neighborhood.

He had simply ignored David's warning and decided to double down. He pushed the team to move faster. Using the adage that it was better to rip the band-aid off. Looking at the severance envelope still unopened beside him, he finally realized his pride and hubris had overshadowed his better judgment.

Marcus turned onto his street, almost not remembering how he got there. The neighborhood looked the same as it always did, manicured lawns and quiet driveways in front of million-dollar homes. He usually did not drive home during the day, so he was not used to the streets' peace and calm. The complete opposite of Marcus's world right now.

The silence was deafening as he pulled into the garage and turned off the engine. For the first time in years, there was no plan. No turnaround to execute. No board meeting to prepare for. No numbers to chase. His system had failed.

He rested his hands on the steering wheel, thinking about how every playbook he had mastered relied on control, speed, efficiency, and certainty. But it was a new world, and none of his systems had prepared him for the rise of AI in the workforce. Marcus finally opened the car door, walked toward the doorway, and pressed the button to close the garage door.

Three months earlier, inside the glass-walled conference room of Silvergate Capital, Nate Faulkner, Operating Partner, stood before a massive screen, reading the financials that told a sobering story. After years of growth, their prized acquisition had stalled. And worse, no one inside the portfolio company seemed to have a real plan to fix it.

"When we bought it two years ago, the company was printing money," Nate said. "Now their EBITDA's been trending downward for the third quarter in a row. The expenses are outpacing revenue, they are burning through their cash reserves, and their customer churn has doubled."

Dane Ellison, the founding Managing Partner of Silvergate, looked at the screen. He was the kind of investor who didn't like messy turnarounds.

"Remind me again of the timeline," Dane asked. "The founders sold the company five years ago to RTI Capital, which held it for three years. We acquired it after solid organic growth when they had brought in a new CEO."

Nate nodded. "Right. When we bought it, we believed we could squeeze a bit more out of it, integrate one or two companies, and make a nice profit. RTI just rode the momentum the founders created, choosing not to make any investments, so we replaced their CEO with Marcus to do what he does best."

"And?"

Nate sighed. "Marcus did what we wanted him to. He found cost savings and made some structural changes. He also went all in with AI tools. Somewhere in the middle of the drive for efficiency and cost savings, they missed the next product cycle introduction. Innovation slowed to a crawl and was noticeable to customers... and to competitors. It wasn't long before they slipped to number two in the market."

Dane stood, walking slowly toward the floor-to-ceiling windows overlooking the city. "This company used to be known for being first to the market, the first to predict what customers wanted. That's why we chose to buy them. We expected this to be easy money."

"Marcus poured capital into automation. He bought every

shiny object labeled 'AI' and 'efficiency,' but missed the one thing that drove this company's success in the first place: its ability to see the market before anyone else did. They've implemented AI agents, process automation, and bots. The stuff looks great on a pitch deck, but no one's pulling value out of it. In an attempt to capture the ROI, his approach was to cut deep into people. So he laid off dozens, but seemed to forget to figure out how to leverage the new tech," Nate said.

"They missed the cycle," Dane muttered, "while competitors leaped forward."

"Yes. And now, Marcus is working with underutilized technology, and no one seems to know its purpose anymore. I don't believe Marcus has a strategy beyond using his playbook; which I will give him, it has served him well over the years. He is just in over his head with this one. "

They sat considering what to do next.

"So," Dane asked, "what's the play? Replace Marcus?"

"Maybe," Nate said, "but that's just another reset. Another outsider who'll need eighteen months to get up to speed, and we don't have that kind of runway. And honestly? We don't need another operator. We need someone who actually understands the DNA of this company. Someone who understands the customers and market."

Dane raised an eyebrow."Then what? Bring in an overpriced consultant? What do you think our options are?"

He paused, then added, "I know this is unorthodox, but what if we brought the founders back?"

Dane turned with a surprised look on his face. That was not usually a smart thing to do. Yes, Apple did it with Jobs, but many founders struggle when they return to their original seat.

"What were their names again?"

Nate replied, "Richard was the CEO, and Alex was the CFO. They built this from the ground up. They scaled it and created a culture that drove results. As I said, I know it's unorthodox, but they've got more institutional knowledge and strategic clarity than anyone else we could find. Bring them in for an advisory role, just to take a look and see what's really going on."

Dane asked, "Do you think they'd say yes?"

"I suspect they'll listen," Nate replied. "Especially if they care about the legacy. I asked around, and Richard has not jumped back into the workforce, while Alex has been doing fractional work for a while."

Dane nodded. "Call Marcus first. He deserves to know where our decision is."

Chapter Two
Called Back

"Captain, we're losing containment in Sector 7. The computer systems are rerouting power, but it's not holding."

The starship bridge was alive with red alerts and crew attempting to diagnose and remedy the issue. A holographic interface hovered in front of the captain, displaying a variety of charts, system diagrams, and diagnostics. Next to it hovered the artificial intelligence system called Nora, projected as a calm, translucent assistant.

"Recommend a course of action, Nora," the captain said, in a steady, concerned voice.

The AI's reply was calm, layered with synthetic empathy, "Vent the auxiliary bay. Divert life support to reinforce primary power. Risk to the crew is minimal. However, the risk to the mission will be catastrophic if you delay beyond three minutes."

The captain hesitated.

"Make the call, sir," said his second-in-command.

The captain's eyes moved between his number one and the screen. "Execute your recommendations, Nora."

The ship shuddered as Nora moved into action. Venting the auxiliary bay caused the starship to shake, and everyone grabbed hold of something close until the stabilizers kicked in. The lights dimmed as power was diverted to the primary power source, allowing the crew to continue their mission."

Bzzzt. Bzzzt.

Richard blinked, pulled out of the page. The starship disappeared, replaced by the warm early light of morning pouring across his living room. The starship was gone; now it was just paper, coffee, and the ringtone again. Bzzzt.

He picked up his phone. "Good morning."

"Saved any galaxies lately?" Alex's voice came through, half laughing.

Richard smiled. "You know me. Always the hero."

"Good morning," Alex replied. "It's been a while."

Richard and Alex had stayed connected. Their families occasionally had a barbecue or dinner out. However, over time, the interactions became fewer and farther apart.

Richard stood, stretching. "How are you, Alex?"

"I'm good. I've been working as a fractional CFO for a couple of mid-sized companies. I can't say it's very exciting, but I haven't found anything else to throw myself into…Yet!"

"Yet. That is the operative word, isn't it? Sounds like you haven't slowed down much."

"Not really. Not wired for too much downtime, I guess."

"So, what do I owe the pleasure of a call? Want to grab a round of golf?"

Alex paused. "I got a call from a new PE group. They acquired our old company."

Richard raised an eyebrow. "Really? Wow, I guess it has been five years since we sold the company." Five years since we walked away, on our terms. The private equity firm they sold to had promised investment, innovation, and global reach.

"Yeah, new ownership, new team, and different operating principles. They're evaluating what they've bought and have serious concerns."

"And they called you?"

"Yes. They said they're looking to steady the ship and asked if we'd consider coming back to help."

It was highly unusual for new owners to seek out the previous founders for help with their purchase. With a look of confusion on his face, Richard moved to the window, coffee in hand. "You thinking about it?"

"Only if you are willing to join me on this new adventure. I told them I wouldn't move forward without talking to you first. I have no interest in jumping back in without you. Especially into the familiar territory of our old company."

"Did they say what the issues are?"

"Not in detail. Just that they're trying to assess the current state, and it sounded like they want a second opinion, or maybe just someone who knows the DNA."

Richard took a deep breath. The world outside seemed far removed from starships and tactical AIs, but maybe it wasn't so different. Systems are breaking down, and decisions need to be made.

"What do you think, Richard? You in?" Alex asked.

Richard didn't answer right away. He took a sip of coffee and stared off into the distance.

"I am intrigued. It's a highly unusual request, as you are well aware of. The PE firms usually have all of the answers. So, why not? Let's meet with them and hear what they have to say," he said. "If nothing else, we get to see each other, but I'm not committing to anything. Honestly, I am more interested in why they would call us."

"Fair enough," Alex replied. "I was wondering the same thing. Leave it to me, I'll set it up."

Richard ended the call and looked back at his book, which he had left on the chair. The book was still open. The captain was in the middle of a crisis. He thought about the AI's words—risk to mission: catastrophic.

Richard thought that fact and fiction were colliding, and it piqued his interest.

Looking at his now-empty coffee mug, Richard walked to the kitchen to pour another cup. While pouring, he spoted Kathy outside and decided to pour her a mug.

Richard walked over to where Kathy was seated on the patio. He handed her one mug and took the chair beside her.

"Alex?" She asked.

"Yeah."

"How's he doing?"

"Oh, he's busy with fractional CFO work."

"Was he looking for a golfing partner or to make dinner plans?" Kathy asked.

"No, I wish. Oddly enough, Alex received a call from a PE firm."

"PE firm? Which one and what did they want? Were they asking about your old company?"

"Kind of. A new PE firm bought it. The call was from the new owners. They want our help to take a look under the hood."

"Both of you?"

Richard smiled and gave a *mhmm* in response. Kathy looked at him with a questioning look as if to ask him what he thought about that.

He took a deep breath and said, "I told him I'd meet with them."

"Really?"

"I am more interested than anything else. So, for now, just a meeting," Richard said, slowly shaking his head yes, trying to process the conversation and its potential impact.

Kathy took a sip of coffee, studying him. "You miss it, don't you. I know you enjoy the peace around here and your books, but at least a part of you must miss it."

"Some days."

"The leadership? Or the purpose?"

He considered that. "Maybe both. It's different now. I think most of the leadership team has moved on, which is common when you have a new CEO. Also, the problems are bound to be different. The tools are different."

"Sounds like they need you and would benefit from your wisdom."

Richard looked at Kathy. "Would you be okay with that? Me stepping back in?"

"If you're doing it to solve real problems, not to chase old ghosts, then yes. Just... don't try to fix everything by yourself."

He reached over and took her hand.

"I am just going to have a conversation at this point. I don't have enough information to determine whether I can help them. Besides, I'm not sure I want to come out of retirement."

They sat quietly as the breeze moved through the trees,

rustling the leaves like a soft applause.

Inside, his book still lay open on his chair—the captain mid-crisis. The AI calmly offering data, choices, and risks.

Risk to mission: catastrophic.

It could be a warning, or maybe it was just a story. Richard couldn't help thinking about that phrase. In every good sci-fi story, it came down to people, to leadership, and a determination to survive. Was this a new mission he should even undertake? He wasn't sure.

That afternoon, Richard received a follow-up email from the PE firm, a calendar invite, and a few company files to review.

"Thank you for agreeing to meet. We look forward to getting your perspective."

Richard responded with a simple: "Same here. We will be there."

He opened the documents, scanning through recent articles and quarterly reports. He found the press release about the acquisition to be boilerplate, with language about synergy and growth potential. Then he found a few scattered headlines about layoffs, restructuring, and a "bold digital transformation strategy."

He clicked through an interview with the new Chief Automation Officer, who spoke about their AI deployment and process automation. Her language was polished, clearly practiced, and she seemed comfortable in front of a camera. What stood out to Richard was the lack of mention of the employees. No sign that anyone had asked the workforce what was working and what wasn't.

Richard closed his laptop. Then he stood, stretched, and walked toward the garage. He had no idea what kind of mess they were walking into.

If there was one thing he and Alex had learned over the years, it was that no system, no technology, no transformation could ever work if it left the human being behind.

A lingering question came to mind. What kind of mess had they gotten themselves in?

Chapter Three
Built to Be Efficient

Driving into the parking lot brought back many memories for Richard, most of them good. He and Alex had built this company from nothing. They, too, had a rough spot where Richard needed to completely rethink how he ran the company. When he did, the company began making record profits and caught the attention of a PE firm. After selling it to the PE buyer, he didn't look back, not really. It took him a few weeks to truly let go, but once he did, he started to look forward to the next adventure.

He spent the last five years trying to find himself. He was a driven person by nature, and filling the void of work was a challenge. He played golf, went on trips, and spent a lot of time with the kids. Eventually, he found a rhythm that suited him. Of everything he considered throwing himself into, coming back to his old company was nowhere on that list.

It felt strange to pull into the visitor parking space, but he did so anyway, took a deep breath, and got out of the car. Upon entering the building, he realized he would not just be able to walk in, especially since he didn't recognize the receptionist sitting behind the desk. Richard gave his name and looked over to see Alex sitting patiently in an armchair.

The receptionist told Richard to wait a few minutes, so he walked over and tapped Alex on the shoulder. A bit surprised, Alex jumped out of his seat and had to laugh when he realized it was Richard.

"Richard, it's great to see you," Alex leaned in to hug him.

"Same here. How long have you been waiting?"

"I just got here a few minutes ago. I'm sure they will be down in no time."

Just as Alex spoke, the new executive assistant approached and asked them to follow her. They went to the fourth floor, and she showed them to the boardroom, not realizing they knew precisely where it was. The boardroom hadn't changed much in five years. Same oversized mahogany table. Same frosted glass walls to create a sense of openness. The same art hanging on the walls as an artifact of the olden days.

"I never liked that picture," Richard whispered to Alex, who looked at it and smiled.

While the room was the same, the faces were different.

Nate stood near the far wall, arms crossed, watching the room like a chess player tracking every move. He was the PE partner from Silvergate Capital—the group that had acquired the company two years ago. Mid-forties, sharp suit, disarming smile that didn't quite reach his eyes.

"Richard. Alex." Nate's voice was smooth and clipped. "It's nice to meet you in person. Glad you made it."

He turned to the room. "For those who haven't met them, Richard is the former CEO, and Alex was his CFO. They're here at my invitation. They've navigated workforce transformation before—and we need that expertise now."

Nate looked at everyone's faces and made introductions after he and his guests took a seat.

"At the head of the table is Marcus, the current CEO," he nodded with an expression that hovered somewhere between polite disinterest and evident irritation. He didn't stand.

"To Marcus's right is Emily. She is the CFO. I think you know David, the COO."

David stood and extended a hand to Richard and Alex with a small but genuine smile. "Good to see you again." He was the only remaining executive from Richard's original leadership team. Time had added some silver to his hair, but the warmth was the same.

"David," Richard replied, shaking his hand firmly. "Glad you're still here."

"Across from David is Brianne, the new chief automation officer." Brianne was young, sharp-eyed, and impeccably dressed. Richard recognized her from the video he saw.

"Next to her is Carlos, the chief commercial officer." He leaned back in his chair with a confident ease. He wore a navy blazer over a t-shirt and sneakers; startup casual in a legacy setting. He offered a quick smile.

"I don't think you have met Julie, either. She is the new CHRO." She gave Richard and Alex a nod and welcomed them.

Marcus didn't bother hiding the tension in his jaw. Noticing this, Nate added, "They're not here to take over," with just enough of an edge to imply Marcus lost the debate with Silvergate about bringing Richard and Alex in. "They're here to help us figure out what's working, what's not, and how to get back on track."

Richard nodded, scanning the faces. Some open. Some closed. Some skeptical.

"It is nice to meet everyone. Shall we get started?" Richard said, leaning forward, "Why don't you tell us what's broken?"

The silence that followed was heavy. He scanned the table again, noting a few familiar expressions. Carlos played with his Montblanc pen as if it were a power move. Marcus furrowed his brow and crossed his arms. Julie looked like she could talk culture all day, but hadn't spent time on the floor in years. And Brianne seemed eager to prove the future was already here, whether or not anyone else was ready. Richard could tell it would be a challenging journey getting them to open up and work together.

Alex sat to Richard's left, looking through a small black notebook. He'd always been more analog than digital, and Richard liked that about him.

"Before we get into anything formal," Nate began, pausing to look at Richard, "I want to thank you for making the time. I know we're all busy. I am sure you all know about the founders, and who better to help us in our current situation? I invited them here to understand the current state of the business. That's it. No decisions, no assumptions. Just a conversation."

A beat passed. Then David leaned forward.

"I can start. Richard, Alex, you will be happy to know we've made quite a bit of progress in the last five years, with significant investments in operational automation. Quality has never been better. Our new digital workflows and AI implementations in core customer processes are ensuring our customer service stays on top of things. The business is evolving."

"That is great," Richard said evenly. "What else has changed since Alex and I stepped away?"

Carlos jumped in, "We digitized the sales pipeline. We are now leveraging predictive analytics to guide our deal flow, and we're spending less time on low-probability leads."

Emily followed, "We rolled out agentic AI across the order-to-cash process. AI now handles the invoicing processes, PO matching, and even some credit analysis for new suppliers."

"HR followed a similar path," Julie chimed in. "Recruiting is largely automated now, with AI tools sourcing potential candidates and the initial outreach. It also handles the first candidate screening and scheduling interviews for those who pass the first step. Our time-to-fill rate is down by forty percent."

Richard listened. They were saying all the right things. Efficiency. Innovation. Optimization. But something felt off.

"And how are those systems performing?" he asked.

The room fell silent as the executives looked at each other, trying to figure out who would speak first.

"They're... functional," Brianne said. "We've had some bumps with implementation and usage. There are certainly exceptions that require manual intervention, but overall, we're moving in the right direction."

"Define 'right direction,'" Richard said.

Blank stares and side eye glances filled the room. No one answered.

Alex said, "Let me come at it differently. Since these systems went live, what have you seen in terms of productivity gains? Cost efficiency beyond headcount? New capabilities? Innovation velocity?"

"We've reduced headcount," David offered.

"Beyond headcount reduction, David," Richard smiled at him. "That's really just subtraction."

Another pause. Julie shifted in her chair uncomfortably.

Brianne cleared her throat. “Look,” she said, “the reality is that some teams have struggled with the adoption, making it pretty bumpy. The workforce hasn’t exactly embraced the changes.”

Richard raised an eyebrow. “Why do you think that is?”

Uncomfortable, Emily folded her arms. “Honestly? Resistance to change and stubbornness about seeing a new path. It comes down to a mindset issue. We’ve provided the tools to improve everything; unfortunately, the people just aren’t adapting.”

Alex jotted something in his notebook. Richard looked around the room.

“Let me make sure I understand,” he said. “The technology works, the strategy is sound, and the tools are implemented well, but the primary constraint is the people?”

A few heads nodded, but no one said a word.

Richard leaned back, considering what they had just said. “Interesting.”

He let that hang in the air.

Then he leaned forward again. “Let me ask you a few questions,” he said, attempting to be measured and deliberate. “Since these changes rolled out, what’s happened to voluntary attrition?”

Everyone looked at Julie, who said, “It has gone up.”

“How many roles have fundamentally changed without being redefined?” he continued. “How many managers were asked to cut heads without having a clear path to getting the work done? And do employees understand why the decisions were made to bring in AI? Have you done any change management or communication initiatives?”

“Look,” Marcus finally spoke up. “We all know that jobs and role changes are unavoidable. The thing you need to understand is that it is not the same business you led five years ago. If we stopped to redefine every role before making a move, we’d still be talking about transformation instead of executing it.”

He glanced around the table, looking for agreement. A few heads nodded.

“As for managers,” he continued, “we didn’t ask anyone to cut heads without a plan. We gave them the tools necessary to pick up the work. The expectation was that technology would absorb the work. That’s the whole point of investing in AI.”

Richard didn't interrupt, so Marcus went on, "And yes, we've talked about why we're bringing AI in. We held town halls, sent out a fair number of emails, and tasked our leaders with cascading it to their teams. I was very clear that we are under significant market pressure. It is clear to everyone that we needed efficiency, to get more done with fewer people."

Alex shifted. "Do they know what it means for them?"

Marcus exhaled. "They know the jobs are evolving, the same as they always are. It should not be a surprise to them. Do they know their job is secure? No. Employees just need to get the work done."

He paused to calm himself down, "I won't pretend everyone loves it, but change is messy, and sometimes it means not everything is clear."

The room stayed quiet.

Alex then asked, "What are the conversations when leadership isn't around? How can we get that filtered to you or the executive team? Or are you flying blind to what the rank and file really think?"

Marcus hesitated and said, "Of course, there's anxiety, which is natural when you introduce large-scale change. Turnover is at the industry standard, so it's not like it's so disruptive that the business is cratering."

"We've been clear to the employees," Marcus continued, "AI is here to help us be competitive and achieve our goals. We see it as freeing teams to focus on higher-value work. We can't stop moving because some people are uncomfortable. Leadership has to make the tough calls, even when they are not popular."

Nate had been listening without interruption while multitasking on his phone. When Marcus finished, he didn't respond right away.

"I don't disagree with the direction," Nate said calmly. "We had to improve EBITDA and grow the company. Introducing AI seemed like a good strategy, especially since standing still wasn't an option."

Marcus nodded, relieved—just slightly.

"But I want to separate direction from results," Nate continued, "because from where I sit, those aren't lining up as I expected. I am not seeing the effort fall to the bottom line."

The room shifted.

He turned toward Marcus. "Saying 'the tools are there' doesn't answer the question of where the results are."

Nate glanced at Richard and Alex, then back to the group. "From an investor standpoint, I care about the bottom line and cash flow. Are we delivering more value now than a year ago?"

He paused.

"If productivity gains are coming primarily from headcount reduction," he said evenly, "that's a short-term story. You aren't building capability if the other value levers are not working properly."

Marcus opened his mouth, then closed it again.

Nate finished quietly, "Something with this strategy to leverage AI isn't adding up. Profits and growth are down; customer complaints, attrition, and other costs are up, while headcount costs are down and technology costs are up. All of this is why I am here and brought Richard and Alex."

Sensing there was nothing left to say, Richard and Alex let the conversation end there. Besides, they didn't want to get into a debate. They were there to learn. The executive team was also happy when the conversation moved on. The team then dug into operations, market position, and strategic direction.

After two hours of dissemination and discussion, Richard sat for a moment to gather his thoughts. He looked around the room.

"Before we wrap," he said, "let me make sure we're hearing you correctly. What I heard today is that a lot has changed since Silvergate took over. You've invested heavily in automation and AI, which sped up the core processes. Some tasks are more efficient, and you lowered headcount. It seems like a lot of the operations are more efficient, at least on paper."

Marcus nodded. "That's accurate," he said.

"I also heard that many of these systems, while functioning, are not fully utilized. Those exceptions still require manual work, and the productivity gains are hard to find on the P&L, beyond the headcount reductions. I also heard that everything implemented should have transformed the organization; however, you have not seen the expected results. "

Alex leaned in slightly. "I heard that those changes haven't always been heard or absorbed by the teams doing the work."

Marcus jumped in, trying not to be defensive, "That's normal in any transformation. You don't flip a switch and get perfection."

Richard looked around the table. "I also heard that AI was the key direction for the company, but the people are struggling to adapt, and that resistance to change is the catch-all for why the transformation is not working out as planned."

A few heads nodded at that last statement.

Richard stopped and looked around. "If we missed something, please let us know."

The executive team looked at each other and had a collective shrug, as if to say that Richard and Alex had a good grasp of the situation.

With that, Richard nodded once. "Alright. I want to thank everyone for their time today. It was definitely insightful."

As the meeting ended, Richard and Alex walked out of the room together. Nate told them he would catch up with them later; he needed to discuss some things with Marcus.

Once the elevator doors closed, Alex asked, "What do you think?"

Richard stared straight ahead. "I think they installed a self-playing piano," he said, "and blamed the audience for not dancing."

Alex smiled faintly. "So? Are we stepping in to help?"

Richard exhaled. "Let me talk to Kathy, and we can catch up in the morning."

That evening, the kitchen smelled like garlic and rosemary. Kathy stood at the stove, stirring a pan, waiting for Richard to join her. She had heard him come into the garage.

"How was it?" she asked, without turning around.

"It was... interesting," Richard said, setting his phone on the counter. "They've put in a lot of tech and automation. Shiny stuff. Agentic AI, bots, and dashboards. But the place feels hollow. They seem to think they have done everything right, and that it's the people who are not using the technology properly who are at fault. They reduced headcount without thinking about the ramifications on those who are left to play with their new tools."

"It sounds like a challenge you would be great at solving.

What are you thinking?"

"Not sure."

She turned, leaning against the counter. "You've been reading more science fiction lately. Maybe that was a precursor to being comfortable attacking a problem with people and technology?"

"Hmm, I don't know. It was strange being back in the building. It was mostly the same, but the atmosphere and faces were vastly different, almost like an alternate universe," he said. Then he paused. "But, there is something here that is intriguing to me. I think it might be fun to see if I still have what it takes to lead the change."

She laughed and shook her head, grinning. "What would it take to fix it?"

"It seems like a whole lot of change management," he said, "but people may be at the heart of it. I would like to speak with Olivia before making any final decisions. It's like I have the answer on the tip of my tongue, but it is just out of reach. I can understand why the current executive team hasn't figured it out. I also am not sure the CEO is up to the task of finding out. Understanding his future will need to be a key question for the PE firm before we get started."

"Sounds like it could be a lot."

"It would be, but I won't go back unless I can do it right."

She reached over and squeezed his hand.

The next morning, Richard and Alex met for breakfast at a quiet cafe tucked between a bakery and an old bookstore. They ordered coffee and eggs, then got to work.

"They don't have a talent problem," Alex said. "They have a leadership vacuum."

"Fascinating. I hadn't thought of it that way. Now that you mention it, a leadership vacuum certainly is part of the issue. I can't help but think there is something else. They may have a talent issue. Besides David, I didn't see anyone that I recognized," Richard stated matter-of-factly and took a bite of his eggs.

"That means they probably also have a culture issue. It seems they have decided to run the company on bots and automation instead of trust," Richard added.

"What's the play?"

"We can't fix it with systems. They've already spent too much time and money changing them. We need someone who understands the people side and the tech side."

"Olivia?"

Richard nodded. "Think she's available?"

"Let's find out."

They called. Olivia answered on the third ring.

"Alex," she said in an honestly excited tone.

"Good morning, Olivia. I have Richard with me. You are on speaker," Alex said, letting her know they were both there.

"What's this? A reunion tour?"

"Something like that," Richard said. "You in town?"

"Actually, yes. A consulting gig wrapped up early. I've got time."

"Are you available for lunch? Our treat."

"Why not?" Olivia said. "I would love to see you. Besides, this must be interesting if the two of you are together and calling me."

The restaurant they selected was quiet with sunlight filtering through linen-draped windows. Olivia arrived exactly on time, sharp in a cobalt blazer, data pad under one arm.

After exchanging pleasantries, they caught up on family, books, and old war stories. Then Alex shifted gears.

"We're looking at going back in," he said. "The company's changed hands, and a new PE group is not happy with their results. They implemented technology everywhere without achieving any significant results. Unless you count reducing headcount to help pay for the implementations."

"What's the diagnosis?" she asked.

"We haven't been able to do a full-blown diagnostic; however, innovation has slowed, employee morale has dropped, and attrition has increased," Richard said. "Instead of figuring out the root cause, they have created a new culture where the treatment for everything is more automation, AI, agents, and bots."

"I can certainly understand the rush into the new world of AI, but the patient blaming the nurses for being sick seems backward," Olivia guessed.

Richard smiled. "Exactly."

"What do you know about the Third Workforce?"

"I've never heard of it," Richard said, turning to Alex. "Have you?" Alex shook his head.

"It's the ecosystem we're already living in," Olivia continued. "The first workforce is your employees. If I were to use HR terminology, I would call them W-2 employees. The second workforce consists of contractors, gig workers, and global freelancers. While we have used temporary labor and contractors for some time, gig workers and freelancers have taken center stage to assist with specific, time-bound projects.

"But the Third Workforce? That is something completely new. This is everything in the metaverse. It encompasses AI, automation, anticipatory analytics, and intelligent digital agents. It is all of the systems, tools, and capabilities that are redefining work itself, and most companies are treating it like software."

"And that's the core issue?" Richard asked.

"It needs to be thought of as a teammate, not just a tool. Until leaders reframe how they think about talent, they'll keep investing in tech and blaming people."

Alex looked at Richard and then turned back to Olivia. "Wait a second. You said, teammate?"

"Yes, we must view all of this new technology as a co-worker and make sure that people are at the center of everything it does. Most research figures that these new capabilities will be able to take on about 30% of the work–the transactional, necessary, but non-value-added work that bogs employees down. Imagine being able to reallocate the right people to strategic activities that will propel the organization forward, instead of them being slaves to the tyranny of tactical and repetitive tasks."

"I am going to have to digest that concept. I trust you, but boy, it seems far-fetched," Alex stated.

Richard smiled, remembering where he left off in his latest book he was reading. He said, "Maybe I have been reading too much science fiction lately, but it makes complete sense to me."

Richard looked at Olivia, realizing that she would be critical to the team's success. "Let's do it. Olivia, what about you? Are you up for another challenge with us?"

"I think this will be fun," she said with a big smile on her face. Alex didn't need to wait. He picked up his phone and called the PE firm.

"We're in," he said. "But we're doing this our way. Marcus can't be a hindrance. If he gets in the way, we will need you to step in. Also, we have a third member of our team that we need to bring to the table."

Richard and Olivia listened to one side of the conversation, knowing that Alex would make sure to cover all the details necessary for this endeavor to succeed. He hung up and looked at them.

"What's our first step?"

Olivia smiled and said, "We start with the Trek."

Chapter Four
The Tension You Can't See

That evening, Richard sat across from Kathy on their back patio to enjoy the early night sky. They had cleared the dinner plates and built a fire in the small stone pit between them. The evening in Texas was warm, and they enjoyed the early autumn sunset.

"It's surreal being back. Like being invited to a dinner party at your old house—same walls, different furniture. Almost everything has changed on the surface. Meeting with Alex and Olivia made it clear that it is a people issue…again," he said.

Kathy took a deep breath. "That sounds exhausting."

"Definitely, but also strangely energizing. I realized I missed it. I don't think I realized how much until now."

"Will you take the job?"

"We already did," Richard said, smiling at her.

She tilted her head. "What made you say 'yes'?"

Reflecting on her question, Richard thought for a moment before answering, "I think the more appropriate question is, why would I say no? And to that question, I really can't think of anything. It will be fun to get back into the game with Alex again. He was such a big part of my work life, and we have drifted apart these last few years after we let go of the company."

Kathy looked into the fire for a moment and said, "If you ask me, I think your heart needed this. Your mind just hadn't completely caught up to the fact that it would give you a lot of joy to step back into the game."

They looked at each other, and he chuckled softly. "You're probably right, as always. What about you? You haven't said much about your day. Should I take that to mean you don't want to talk about it? Which means you really should."

Kathy let out a sigh that said more than words. "You could say that." Kathy's stare returned to the fire.

Kathy hadn't planned to re-enter the workforce. When Richard sold the company, it was the first time they could both fully exhale. She left teaching behind with a sense of peace, not loss. Their days slowed. They traveled with their kids during school breaks, spent long afternoons on the back patio reading and sipping wine, and eased into a rhythm that felt earned. It felt more like arriving at a destination than retiring.

So when her old friend called to talk about the opportunity, it was a cause that Kathy couldn't ignore. She did not realize she was looking for purpose in her life. She wasn't unhappy, but since she and Richard retired, it felt like they had been floating in place, in stasis. She realized she longed to engage with something bigger than herself.

Her friend had joined a nonprofit called CI, short for Children International, which supported children in under-resourced regions worldwide. She had the opportunity to speak with donors about building schools, reuniting families, and equipping leaders to care for vulnerable children in their communities. It stirred something in Kathy; maybe it was the teacher or the mother in her. Whatever part it was, the mission of doing good for vulnerable children made her feel alive.

At first, Kathy replaced her full-time teaching with volunteering. She started by writing thank-you notes, helping out at donor events, and reviewing letters from field employees to categorize them for the team. As she listened and learned, she naturally began to make things better. She spotted gaps and filled them. She offered suggestions that improved things, and she fixed small inefficiencies that most had just accepted. Before long, the

CEO and others in leadership began to notice.

When a position on the development team opened up, her friend asked if she'd consider applying. Kathy laughed at first.

"I've never raised a dollar in my life," she said, however, she had a vast network and a genuine belief in the cause.

After talking it through with Richard over a weekend that included long walks, pros-and-cons lists, and a lot of "what ifs," she said yes.

The learning curve was steep, but Kathy learned fast.

Within months, she had built a new donor welcome strategy, rewritten the foundation grant templates, and designed a quarterly impact newsletter. Major donors loved the changes, and it showed in the giving. Her former students, now professionals and parents themselves, responded to her outreach. "If you're working with them, I'll support it," they said. Over the years, her relationships had built a natural donor base for her to engage.

She brought in several new corporate sponsors in her first year and developed a monthly giving campaign that exceeded its annual goal in just six months. Her work was meticulous, thoughtful, and effective.

Which was precisely why her CEO kept giving her more.

"You've got capacity," she said one day after a staff meeting, "and you're good at solving problems. Would you mind helping out with the upcoming site visit logistics, too?" Kathy didn't mind at first. She did have capacity and was happy to be of service, even though it went beyond her immediate job description.

Then came the website overhaul. And the donor database cleanup. And heading up a board retreat planning committee. And then an interim team lead role when the program director went on leave. By the end of her second year, Kathy had become a go-to for nearly everything that mattered and for many things that shouldn't have landed on her desk at all.

But she didn't complain. She liked being the person that everyone could rely on, even if it meant she put in more time than others. She felt seen, known, and appreciated, which was not always the case when she was teaching. There were times she complained to Richard that she needed to do a better job at setting boundaries. However, she cared so deeply for the mission that those complaints didn't last long. Despite occasional feelings of being overwhelmed, she loved the work, especially the parts that brought her closer to the mission: visiting field sites, mentoring junior staff, and sharing stories that inspired others to care about it.

The children were the heartbeat of it all. Kathy kept photos of several she had met on donor trips tucked into her planner. She remembered all of their names. Every time she looked at the pictures, it brought a smile to her face and reminded her why she worked there in the first place. She loved collecting the children's stories and sharing them with donors and anyone who would listen. The stories of the children they were helping grounded her when she got sucked into spreadsheets and campaign metrics.

Lately, though, the job had been changing.

She turned to Richard, weariness evident in her voice, "You know how we've been piloting new programs at CI? Trying to expand our reach without losing the relational part?"

He nodded.

"Yesterday, we had a meeting with our director of operations. She introduced a whole slate of new AI tools she wants us to implement. Some brand-new technologies include automated grant writers, intake chatbots for new students, and predictive analytics for student success. Guess who's supposed to lead the rollout?" She raised her hand with a sarcastic smile. "Yours truly."

Richard raised his eyebrows. "That sounds... exciting?"

She shook her head. "Not so much. It feels like we're selling our souls to the devil. We work with kids, Richard. Real kids. Many of them have gone through unthinkable trauma. You don't connect with them through automation."

Richard was quiet, giving her space.

She went on, "I know these changes could help us reach more people, but I didn't join CI to become a systems analyst. I joined to help kids, to engage others in the work they are doing, and even to hug them. AI doesn't see people, Richard."

Richard took another moment before replying, "What's your boss saying about it?"

"She says we have to evolve or risk losing donors. Foundations want measurable outcomes and streamlined reporting. We'll free up time for more connection by letting the tech handle the rest, but it doesn't feel that way. It feels like a new fad of replacement therapy."

"You're worried it's replacing the soul of the work?"

She nodded.

Richard looked at Kathy. "You know, at the office today, I saw something similar. Everyone was talking about automation, AI, and cost savings, but no one was talking about people. There's an assumption that technology will fix the problem, but it has created a new kind of challenge, one that's more subtle."

Kathy smiled sadly. "Maybe we're both being pulled into this new world whether we want it or not."

He shook his head, looking thoughtful, "Maybe, or maybe we get to decide how we walk into it."

She leaned over, resting her hand on his. "I just don't want to lose the parts of my work that matter most to me."

"Neither do I," he said. "Which is why it has to be on our terms, and maybe we figure out how to walk into this next chapter together. You with your kids. Me with this broken company. Both of us are trying to keep the human part alive."

Kathy's hand lingered on his for a moment, the quiet between them was comfortable. The sun was gone now, and the last trace of light left the edges of the trees glowing.

She looked at him. "Do you know where you'll start?"

Richard exhaled, leaning back in his chair. "That's the question, isn't it?"

She tilted her head, waiting.

"Olivia brought something up today. She said we need to begin with a new version of the Talent Trek."

Kathy's smile returned, "That sounds familiar."

"It is. In name, at least," he said. "But it's different this time. The workforce is different. The tools, the pace, the expectations—it's more than putting the right people in the right roles. I think we need to revise what even is a team."

She raised an eyebrow. "What's the new version of the trek?"

"Overall, it has a lot of similarities to the original trek. It layers in some new stops along the journey. Olivia said we'll need to map out how humans, AI, and external talent work together to make us a better organization. We need to start rethinking job roles, redesigning workflows, and preparing leaders to manage ecosystems. Honestly, I have a lot to learn, and while it is intriguing to me, I need to get a better handle on this idea."

Kathy looked for the right words, "That sounds big."

"It is. Olivia's point was simple: if we don't lead this intentionally, the system will default to cost-cutting and chaos. The tech will take over, not because it's better, but because no one bothered to tell it how to help."

Kathy gave a wry smile, "Sounds a little like my situation."

"I think we're both facing the same shift, just from different sides. You're to lead AI integration without sacrificing human connection, and I need to reimagine a workforce that's already fractured and drifting from AI integration gone wrong."

They sat in silence for a few moments, both absorbing the weight of their situation.

He shifted in his chair and glanced at Kathy, who was now staring ahead, quietly thinking again.

"You remember that night back in Cleveland?" he said softly. "We were recently married, and we stayed up until two in the morning deciding if I should take that operations manager role? This was before I met Alex and we started the company."

She nodded, "I remember. It was an awful apartment. We had all those ants, and the floor was slanted, so everything kept shifting over time. "

She leaned back, her eyes shining with the memory. "It was a simpler time. I remember you were unsettled about taking the role, and you kept asking, 'What if I mess it up? What if I'm not ready?' And I remember saying something like, 'Then you learn, and we'll figure it out.'"

He nodded, eyes on her now. "You did say that."

"Well," she said softly, "maybe we're just at another one of those moments."

"Yeah," he whispered. "But this time, it's both of us stepping into something new."

She reached for his hand again and squeezed it gently. "Then we'll learn, and we'll figure it out."

Chapter Five
Everything Looks Fine

Nothing had changed from the week before. The same cloud of heaviness hung over the office as Richard, Alex, and Olivia headed to the conference room for the day's activities. Once there, the three of them took seats near the head of the table as the remaining members of the executive team filed in. Some offered quick nods. Others avoided eye contact altogether.

After a few minutes of polite settling and small talk, Richard stood and faced the group.

"First, I want to thank you for being here, and for the work you've been doing under pressure," he said. "We know the last few months have brought change, and not all of it has been easy. We're not here to point fingers. We're here to figure out what's next and how we move forward to get the results Silvergate needs from you."

He paused, letting the room breathe.

"Before we dive into the details, I want to introduce someone who will help us along our journey. Olivia is an experienced Talent Tactician and is here to help us rethink how we work, lead, and align people- both human and digital- to deliver on our mission. She was instrumental in helping Alex and I rethink what was important when I was still CEO.

"Without her, we would have closed the doors long ago. She helped us realize that people are the competitive advantage of any company. I had never considered that, and when we shifted our mindset, the company took off."

Olivia said, "Thanks, Richard."

Richard continued, "To kick things off today, I asked each of you to prepare a short presentation of the system and tools you have already implemented from a technology standpoint. This is not meant to be comprehensive. Since I heard how proud everyone is of the new systems, I'd like to see them laid out. I would like each of you to focus on what's working, your current AI or automation usage, and what impact you're seeing."

Marcus leaned back and gestured toward Brianne. "Let's start with Brianne. She will be able to give the best overview of our impressive accomplishments."

Brianne looked around the table before starting on her presentation. "We've made significant strides in automation across both compliance and our shared services. We've built out workflows using Power Automate and some Python-scheduled scripts that handle internal audit tracking, documentation reviews, and procurement requests."

She looked at the screen behind her and hit enter. A dashboard featuring real-time compliance statistics appeared.

"We also implemented a virtual assistant that interfaces with our SharePoint and our SOP database. It basically parses keywords and delivers documents instantly. It's good automation, but it is technically not AI. Our employees like the response time."

Olivia nodded, "It sounds like it is a useful tool, but is more of a smart retrieval tool than an intelligent agent?"

Brianne's bravado faltered slightly. "Right now, yes, but it's scalable."

When Brianne finished, Emily took the HDMI cord from her and plugged it into her laptop. "SmartFin, a digital finance agent that sits on top of our ERP, handles about sixty percent of our monthly reporting. I like this tool since it monitors our AP/AR transactions, flags anomalies, and produces a great dashboard with proactive alerts. It essentially is our first layer of activity before anyone in Finance has to step in."

"What about forecasting? Have you made any inroads in being able to predict next month or quarter?" Alex asked.

Emily nodded. "We've begun testing GPT-assisted forecasting prompts, primarily for scenario planning. We believe it has a lot of potential, however, we have not made much progress."

Emily finished and didn't wait to hand the HDMI cord to David. He began, "Operations have been aggressive in implementing AI tools. We've installed fantastic predictive maintenance sensors on seventy percent of our equipment, which alert us to any potential downtime. We now have a nifty digital dashboard that flags variances in output, speed, or quality."

"Is that AI or just real-time monitoring, which has been around a while?" Olivia asked gently.

David shrugged. "It's a rules-based system that uses historical data and trend models. We're exploring opportunities to transition to an AI-based system, but haven't found the right one yet."

Richard raised an eyebrow but said nothing.

"We've also rolled out voice-to-text checklists for our warehouse teams. It guides them through process steps hands-free, boosting productivity eighteen percent; and before you ask, this has an AI backbone," David said with a smile.

Olivia nodded and smiled back. When no one had any questions, David looked at Julie, who smiled faintly and took the cord.

"We, also, have been busy with automation and dabbling with AI tools. We began using AI by integrating our applicant tracking tool into our onboarding process. It walks new hires through documents, FAQs, and training modules," Julie said, clicking through her slides.

"Any AI in talent acquisition processes?" Olivia asked.

"I am getting to that," Julie said. "We then moved to put in a resume screening bot that scans for keywords and allows us to filter out resumes that don't match what we are looking for. It has saved the recruiters a ton of time not having to read all of those resumes. We are also starting to look at AI agents to conduct the team's initial interviews. And, we are also piloting a learning assistant that recommends training paths based on the employee's role and their desired career path. It's still in the early stages, but the pilot group seems to like the functionality."

"What about performance reviews, employee engagement, payroll, or the other HR processes?" Richard asked.

"Only automation, but nothing intelligent yet," she admitted. "On the positive side, we've cut our HR admin staff by nearly a third because of all of our automation and the AI tools we've implemented."

Carlos flashed a big smile when Julie handed him the cord. "Marketing's got the flashiest stuff, of course, and we are farthest along, if I don't say so myself. We're using generative AI for emails and blog outlines, and have jumped into GEO and AEO to ensure the AI engines pull our information. I can proudly say that our campaigns are delivered faster than ever, and the engagement of our socials and websites is up 27% and 22%, respectively."

Alex chimed in and asked, "What is GEO and AEO? Those are new terms for me."

Carlos smirked, as he liked being the smartest person on a topic. "GEO stands for Generative Engine Optimization, and AEO for Answer Engine Optimization. Think of it as SEO for AI tools. It focuses on making our content readable, authoritative, and credible to LLMs like ChatGPT, Claude, and Perplexity.

"Thank you. That is helpful."

Carlos nodded and continued, "We also have an AI agent that looks at customer sentiment, scans customer reviews, and flags risks. It is pretty cool, since it learns the tone and can categorize themes."

He paused. "In addition, you have all seen the AI videos that are out on social media. Some of them are pretty impressive, so we're testing this AI functionality for customer videos. It's early, but I believe it will save a ton on production costs."

Olivia let the silence linger as Carlos unplugged the HDMI cord from his laptop, and the screen went black.

"This is very impressive work," she said genuinely. "You've implemented a tremendous amount of automation and AI across the enterprise."

Marcus folded his arms. "So, we're done here?"

Olivia smiled.

"Not quite," she said. "While you have made a lot of progress, most of what I'm hearing falls into two categories: the first is core automation. Your speed is certainly something to be proud of. The second category is early-stage AI layered on top of it. It appears you have streamlined workflows that speed up your transactional tasks. I can see you're starting to surface insight earlier. However, the tools you've implemented are still dependent on rules, prompts, and human interpretation to carry them across the finish line."

She paused.

"If I were to boil it down to one sentence, it's that you're optimizing the systems you have, but there doesn't appear to be a fully thought-out framework to redesign against."

Olivia let the topic rest as she saw Marcus fume on the other side of the table.

"Before we shift gears," she said, "I have one more question for the group, which may seem simple on the surface, but is essential underneath."

She looked directly at Marcus, "With all of this automation, what change management strategies did you put in place?"

The room went quiet.

Marcus glared at Olivia and said, "We've communicated every change we have made. I don't have the exact number of emails, FAQs, or training sessions. Honestly, Olivia, our people are smart enough to know what's coming. It's not rocket science."

Brianne interjected, "That's right. Most of the tools we implemented were plug-and-play. While we sent a lot of communications, I don't think we really needed a whole change management campaign."

Olivia wore a questioning look as she said, "How did the employees respond?"

Exasperated, Marcus said, "Just stop. If we want to keep up in this market, people need to adapt. They need to adapt fast since we can't afford to spend months coddling our snowflake teams every time we install a new AI tool."

The rest of the leadership team sat in uncomfortable silence. Julie shifted in her seat, Carlos avoided eye contact with everyone, and Emily remained silent, her expression unreadable, as usual.

Olivia nodded slowly. "I understand," she said and then looked at Julie. "Have you conducted any employee feedback sessions or surveys? If so, how are engagement scores trending?"

Marcus's irritation was beginning to bubble to the surface visibly. "We don't have time for soft metrics right now. We are fighting for our jobs and our company's existence. If people need group therapy, they can use their EAP credits."

Olivia glanced at Richard, then back at the team. "I am just trying to get a better understanding of where we're starting, and I guess the answer is no.

"If we want a real transformation–one where we keep our jobs and the company thrives– and not just faster transactions, then the people side of change must be foundational."

There was a heavy pause after Olivia's statement. The room sat with the tension caused by Marcus' earlier statements, no one quite ready to break it.

Finally, Richard cleared his throat and said, "Marcus, I see you are frustrated. The pressure weighs heavily on the leader when the heat's on. I did the same thing, since it's easy to focus on speed, efficiency, and measurable results; but I've also seen what happens when we don't bring people with us, when we treat change like a transaction instead of a transformation."

He gestured toward Olivia. "She is not advocating creating safe spaces for employees or hand-holding them through the change. She wants to make sure the system and processes don't implode when the humans can't keep up."

Alex injected a more analytical point of view, "I've run the numbers on a few of these AI upgrades. The ROI looks promising, but I can see where you are not actually getting the return you expected. It appears work has slowed down while employees try to figure out how to get their work done without the implemented tools. When you manage change well, you see a faster adoption, not quiet resistance."

He paused, scanning the group. "It seems like you have been installing technology, and forgot that you still needed your people to run the business."

Marcus exhaled loudly but said nothing. His jaw was tight, muscles twitching in agitation.

Richard looked around the room again. Faces and eyes followed his sweeping view, some hopeful, some skeptical. "Alex and I have both led turnarounds before. What I've learned the hard way is: you can't cut your way to growth. You have to build trust with the people tasked to lead the transformation. That's what Olivia's trying to surface here."

Olivia nodded in quiet gratitude and said, "Thank you. Now, let's talk about where we go from here."

She plugged the HDMI cord into her laptop, and a slide titled **Where Are We Now?** appeared on the screen.

"I don't have a magic wand to wave over the company," she began. "I do have a lot of questions, though. It is difficult to solve a problem unless we fully understand the situation. From what I've heard so far, there is a lot of work ahead of us and still a lot of unanswered questions."

She clicked to the next slide: a blank screen with four words in bold.

People. Work. Tech. Trust.

"I want to start with some simple questions. I'm not asking for polished answers. I would like each of you to do a gut check and give me honest ones.

"First: how many people have you let go in the last twelve months?"

Julie felt all eyes turn to her. "It's close to eighteen percent of our salaried workforce. If we include contractors, it moves the number closer to twenty-two percent."

Olivia nodded, writing it down.

"Next: Is all the work that used to be done by those people still getting done?"

David spoke after a short pause, "Yes, the work is still getting done because those processes are automated. The remaining employees picked up any leftover tasks. All that to say, a lack of resources has caused unintentional work droppage."

Carlos chimed in, "That is just for operations. Following our cuts, we expanded our territories and added more administrative responsibilities to the sales team, which is certainly causing some grumbling. While our Marketing team is having a hard time keeping up with all of the events, conferences, internal requests, and social media activity, I don't think we dropped anything in my world."

"And who," Olivia asked, "is making those decisions? Who's tracking what got dropped versus what work is still getting done?"

Another pause. The executives looked at each other. David finally spoke up, "We've been making those calls at the team level.

When a supervisor sees an issue, they are quick to address it. If you are asking if we are managing this centrally, well, the answer would be no."

Olivia nodded and clicked again. Another simple slide popped up: **Work Without Workers?**

She turned to the group. "You implemented AI and other automation. You also cut a sizable portion of your workforce. Are you clear about who's doing the work now? Which parts are being handled by people and which by technology?"

No one responded.

She let the silence linger for a minute.

"My next question is, who owns the technology that each function is implementing? Not in the IT sense, rather, who oversees the process and the output? Who is managing the performance and who is ultimately accountable for the results? When a bot misses something, who notices? When AI rewrites your policy manual, who signs off?"

Brianne opened her mouth, then closed it again, lips pursed.

"And lastly: how's morale? Do you understand how employees are feeling about everything?"

The air thickened, dealing the final blow to the facade the team had been building. Shoulders stiffened. Eyes dropped.

Julie answered, hesitantly, "To be honest, people are tired of the extra work we put on them and have a fairly low level of trust in the executive team. There seems to be a bit of confusion around their roles, and a lot of fear about who's next on the chopping block. Some are excited about the AI tools, sure, but most feel like they're doing more with less, without any understanding of the ultimate vision or even what success looks like."

"Thank you for the honesty," Olivia said.

She turned to Marcus and Emily to see their reactions. They both sat there, stoic. Marcus, with his arms crossed. Emily was on her phone. Either doom-scrolling or texting with someone. Though clearly checked out.

Making the mental note, Olivia thought for a minute and said, "What I am hearing is a level of disconnection between this team and the front-line employees. I believe this is where we start. Not to point blame at anyone. Understanding where it's broken allows us to build the right plans to fix it."

Richard watched the executives as they absorbed the reality of their situation. They understood there was a significant disconnection between them and the employee base.

Olivia clicked to the next slide.

At the top of the screen, bold letters read: **Talent Trek 2.0 – Leading the Integrated Workforce**.

Below it, a circular diagram appeared, shaped like a journey with seven way points.

Richard spoke up before Olivia could say anything, "Before we dive in," he said. "I think it's important to remember where we've already been."

The room turned toward him.

"David is the only one of you who was here when we rolled out the original Talent Trek. That framework helped us develop our first talent strategy, which clarified the value of aligning top talent with critical roles. Feeding into succession planning that drove business growth. This process gave us much better visibility to our top talent across the entire enterprise, so we could leverage them to solve some of our biggest issues."

Richard continued, "What Olivia is about to walk us through is the next-generation version. Though it never hurts to run through the original trek from time to time. It is amazing how quickly the world has changed in the last five years. Which means business is more complicated, and getting the work accomplished takes more than employees. We must figure out how to manage a whole new ecosystem of employees, contractors, and bots in a distributed team. Since the work gets completed in different ways, our leadership model must evolve to manage it effectively."

He looked toward Olivia. "She is not taking some dusty old management theory off the shelf. However, that could be a good idea for some people. What she is doing is creating something completely new, based on everything we have learned over the last twenty-five years of technological advancement. Think of it this way, we are building the vehicle for where we need to go next, but we are doing so while driving down I-35 at 85 mph."

Olivia nodded in appreciation.

"Well said, Richard. Talent Trek 2.0 builds on the foundation you may be familiar with, which this company walked through several years ago. However, the terrain we're navigating now is far more complex and more interconnected. Let me walk you through the journey we're about to take together.

"As Richard said, we're dealing with a complete workforce transformation scenario. It's going to require every one of us to think and lead differently.

"In the past, we focused mostly on optimizing human potential with tools like talent reviews, succession plans, and development tracks. Don't get me wrong, these tools are still incredibly important for managing full-time employees, but now, we need to reimagine leadership in a world where your 'team' might include contractors, digital agents, AI co-workers, external ecosystems, and employees. The way forward is to build out an integrated workforce."

David crossed his arms. "What do you mean by an integrated workforce, Olivia? You keep saying 'AI co-workers and digital agents,' as if we're hiring them instead of implementing them. What are you really getting at?"

Before Olivia could answer, Emily jumped in, "Look, I get it. We've been using more automation. Are you seriously saying bots are employees now?"

There were a few low laughs around the room. Even Marcus cracked a faint smile.

Olivia didn't blink. She just stood up, walked to the whiteboard, and drew three interlocking circles.

"I'm not saying bots are employees," she said, "but they are doing employee work, and if you don't know what they're doing, who's managing them, and how they fit into your workflow, you may have some significant blind spots."

She labeled the circles as she spoke.

"The First Workforce is your full-time, permanent employees, the people on your payroll. They are the holders of your culture, the ones who remember the stories and collect the company's artifacts. They know how things get done and take pride in their work.

"The Second Workforce is your freelancers, gig workers, contractors, and contingent labor. This workforce gives you a lot of flexibility. They are often specialized to handle very specific projects or tasks, or they may help during peak periods of work. While we have a lot of experience with this workforce, leaving them out of strategic conversations under-leverages their inputs."

Pausing before writing in the final circle, Olivia continued, "The Third Workforce is the new workforce you are integrating into your company. This workforce is your AI, automation, digital agents, bots, and intelligent platforms. It used to be that you implemented a system, CRM, ERP, or any other technology to help manage and automate processes, but humans were still required to use the application or tool.

"Now? These tools are part of your operational system, helping you make decisions, complete tasks, and interact with your employees and customers. When you implemented an ERP, it wouldn't do anything unless a human told it to do the task. Who looks at the results completed by an AI bot now?"

Emily scoffed, "Now your just being silly. Using a bot to screen out candidates or help draft job descriptions doesn't make it part of the workforce."

Olivia responded, "And yet, how many candidates are looked at before AI filters them out? How many job descriptions go live without human review? Who's accountable when the system creates unwanted outcomes? Make no mistake, AI is influencing business outcomes. That makes it part of the workforce whether we like it or not."

Julie nodded slowly, but Marcus shook his head.

"This all sounds like semantics to me," Marcus said. "Why split hairs? We need speed. We need automation if the bots help us do that, great. But humanizing them? It's a complete red herring and consulting speak."

Olivia responded, "I agree in part. We need the automation, but we need to lead it differently than we would an application or ERP system.

"Let's say you deploy a new scheduling AI bot. Its primary function is to prioritize cost-efficiency. What does it do? It cuts hours for your most tenured staff and loads up shifts for low-cost part-timers. Now your culture suffers, turnover increases, quality declines, and customer satisfaction drops. But the AI met its KPI to lower labor costs."

She continued to look Marcus in the eyes. "That's what happens when you implement AI without thinking through the management of the bots. AI has no concept of human nuance.

The design is to optimize, and if you don't set the guardrails, you'll get what it thinks you want, not what your business actually needs. There is no critical thinking in AI. Humans should complete that task."

Carlos spoke up, "Are you really saying we're supposed to treat these tools like coworkers?"

"In reality, they already are co-workers," Olivia said. "Think of it this way: you brainstorm with ChatGPT, your customer service team uses AI chatbots to streamline level one customer queries, and your supply chain dashboards predict outcomes and suggest directions. These systems are now doing the kind of work we used to assign to analysts, coordinators, and interns.

"There is a significant risk when you let AI operate without any oversight. You essentially abdicate leadership. Which has broad-reaching consequences on everything from team morale and culture."

Brianne finally spoke, "What's the alternative? Slow down adoption? We're behind as it is. I say lean in, and add more automation, not less."

Olivia nodded. "No, slowing down is not necessary, but you do need to lead differently; you need to lead better. You wouldn't onboard a new employee without training, assigning a manager, and having a clear set of responsibilities, so why would you treat a system that makes business decisions any differently?"

Emily crossed her arms. "We don't have time to babysit software. Our managers don't have enough time to manage their flesh and blood employees as it is."

"That's the rub, isn't it?" Olivia asked. "At the end of the day, you do need to govern. You need to know what work is being done by machines, what's being done by people, and where the handoffs are. Can you tell me where that is happening here? Are you truly getting the full value out of everything you have done? I think we already have that answer.

"AI really doesn't reduce headcount; it frees up capacity to hire more people with the right skills and competencies to drive growth. That's the opportunity of AI. It will help employees do new things and take the business to new heights, but only if you lead the transformation.

"Here's how I see it. The First Workforce is the foundation.

You need them for culture and critical thinking. The Second gives you flexibility and a focus on skills. The Third gives you scalability. Unfortunately, if they aren't working together, you open the door for a lot of chaos."

Julie cocked her head to the side. "What does that orchestration actually look like?"

Olivia smiled. "I am glad you asked."

She clicked to her next slide, revealing the circular map of the **Talent Trek 2.0**.

"Let me show you the roadmap."

Olivia gestured to the slide now glowing behind her: a

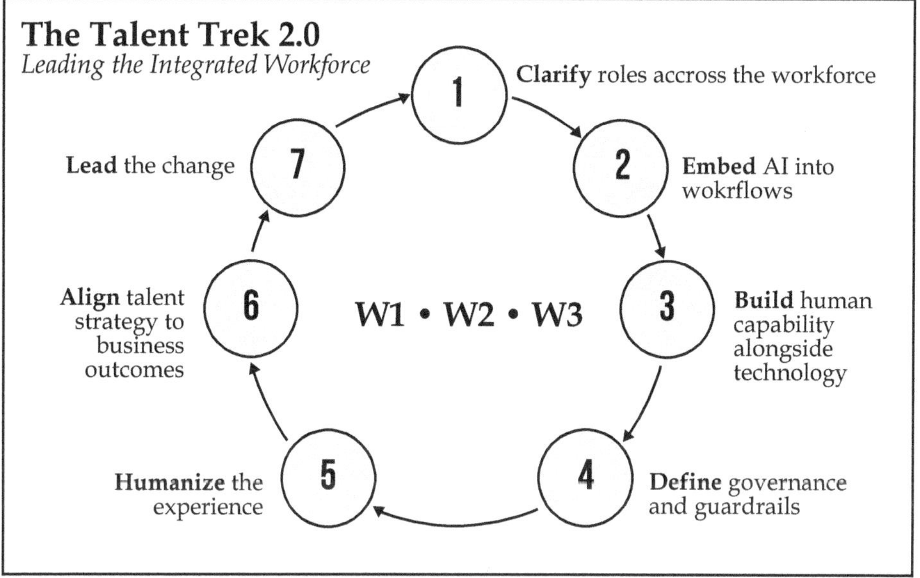

stylized map with seven milestone markers connected by arrows.

"The Talent Trek 2.0 is a structured journey to help organizations like yours transition from workforce confusion to workforce cohesion, especially now that we're dealing with not two, but three different workforces operating simultaneously."

Pointing to the screen, Olivia said, "I want to take you through the stops of the new Talent Trek."

1. Clarify Roles Across the Workforce

"First, we need to map who is doing the actual work across all three workforces. I don't believe anyone has documented which roles are fully human, which are hybrid, and which are digital-first.

"You'd be surprised how many leaders assume something is 'taken care of,' only to find it's fallen through the cracks. Sometimes a burned-out employee drops the ball, sometimes an application is forgotten about, and now sometimes your AI agent is going off the rails. This phase brings everything into the light, providing visibility to the work and aligning all workforces across the whole system."

Carlos nodded his head and said, "I get it. We're really not talking about job descriptions anymore. We are looking at mapping out how each of the workforce elements fits together. Is that it?"

Olivia smiled and said, "That's right. Everyone needs to know their lane and how it connects to the others."

Olivia clicked, and the next bullet appeared.

2. Embed AI Into Workflows

"Next, we move beyond deploying tools and start embedding AI into the actual work. Most of what I heard this morning sounded like isolated components, efficient, yes, but still disconnected.

"Embedding could mean your marketing campaigns leverage predictive analytics, AI augments employee onboarding, and operations simulate production outcomes in real time. It means being thoughtful about your process flow, instead of letting AI bots run around like kittens."

"That's going to require cross-functional redesign," David chimed in.

"That's exactly why it's a trek. It will be a difficult journey. Much more difficult than the original trek you went on a few years ago."

The next bullet appeared at Olivia's prompting.

3. Build Human Capability Alongside Technology

"Third, we must invest in the human side of the transformation. And no, I don't mean another soft skills seminar," she said, glancing at Marcus.

"I'm talking about real training in prompt engineering, AI fluency, digital ethics, and cross-functional collaboration. You should equip your employees for success when they work alongside intelligent systems. You must proactively train them to work effectively with the new tools."

Julie said, "We've done some of that, but it's been patchwork."

"That's fairly common, as most organizations are not thinking across the enterprise. The Talent Trek 2.0 formalizes it so that the organization can get the maximum value out of the investment," Olivia replied and clicked to the next slide.

4. Define Governance and Guardrails

"The Fourth stop is governance. It is critical to know who's monitoring what your systems are doing. You know who's responsible when an AI system makes a questionable decision and what the escalation path should be.

"This phase involves getting very explicit on the ethical, operational, and legal lines and determining ownership. Without it, you certainly risk compliance issues, and worse, a collapse of trust."

"Isn't that an IT responsibility?" Emily asked, almost sincerely.

"It's shared in this new reality. Finance, HR, Ops, Marketing; all of you play a role. It is everyone's responsibility to ensure the company complies and remains under control. All functions must work together to manage the whole ecosystem."

5. Humanize the Experience

"This next step is where most organizations stumble. As we increase our organizations' digital presence, we tend to dehumanize the work. This phase is about restoring that balance. How do we preserve the culture when bots send the first email to a new hire? In this step, we spend the time to preserve the DNA of your company."

Marcus muttered, "Here we go again…"

Without skipping a beat, Olivia replied, "Marcus, I know it sounds touchy-feely or fluffy nonsense. I can tell you that human-centric design has delivered bottom-line results in every high-performing company I've worked with. People need meaning in their work."

6. Align Talent Strategy to Business Outcomes

As the next slide appeared, Olivia said, "Once your workforce understand their expectations, you've established the tools into the ecosystem and you train your employee base, then and only then, you can shift the focus toward strategy alignment. The key questions in this phase are do we have the right skills for where we're going? And does your workforce investments reflect your strategic priorities?"

"This is an interesting way to look at it. Would we start planning people capacity like we do capital?" Brianne asked.

"That is a good way to think about it– strategic workforce architecture– just like you manage supply chains or financial portfolios," Olivia replied.

7. Lead the Change

With a final click, Olivia said, "None of this Trek sticks without training leaders at every level to lead through the ambiguity of significant change. The Talent Trek 2.0 concludes by developing leaders who can coach across teams composed of all three workforces. They must be able to identify issues in blended workflows and maintain a high morale, even when the terrain becomes rough.

"Leadership today is undergoing a significant upheaval. Welcome to the age of the Third Workforce."

Olivia looked around the group. "Those are the stops of the Talent Trek 2.0. Think of the trek as a journey in which each of you plays a role in walking it. If we do this right, we get to reinvent who we are and come out on top."

Richard's eyes swept the room again. No one was checking their phone. No one was disengaged. They were in it. Really in it.

He looked at Olivia and thought that this was more than a map. It was their compass.

Then Marcus leaned forward, folded his hands on the table, and cleared his throat. "I've been listening," he said slowly, deliberately. "Quietly. Because I wanted to see where this would lead."

Richard turned slightly toward him, already bracing.

Marcus continued, his voice was cold, "Here's what I think about all of this… It's a load of crap."

A few heads turned sharply.

"Humanizing technology? Guardrails? Emotional responses to AI? Come on," He shook his head. "We're not building a philosophy department, we're running a business, and the business needs results."

Marcus gestured toward the screen. "Our margins are dropping as our competitors undercut our prices, and it is not getting any easier. The market is tightening though this economic slow down. The only things that'll keep us in the game are speed of execution, and automation to drive cost efficiency. We don't have the luxury of slowing down to see how the employees 'feel' about the new technology."

Emily, seated beside him, didn't speak, but give a nod to what Marcus was saying.

Marcus went on, "If people can't keep up, then they can quit and find another job. I am not going to cower or babysit employees. There are plenty of people who want to work here and are willing to take orders. The only thing we owe them is a paycheck for the work they perform. If we take months to train the ones who can't keep up, they won't have a job at the end of it and will have wasted our time and resources in the process."

A heavy silence followed. The kind that follows when someone finally says what others have been thinking, but didn't dare voice: would they have enough time to implement the changes, any changes, before it's too late, and the company goes under?

Emily finally spoke, "I agree with Marcus. This is not a therapy clinic or a day care. If the tools work, then get over it and use them. If employees can't adapt, then leave. There are plenty of people who would like to work for us. I don't see the upside in spending cycles trying to manage feelings about systems that make us faster."

Across the table, Julie's jaw tightened, but she said nothing.

Carlos exhaled slowly. "Just to be clear, we're saying that efficiency is more important than engagement?"

Emily didn't respond. The answer was already in the air.

Brianne broke in, "I don't really care how people feel about the tech. As I said before, I just want more of it. If we automate something well, we save time. If we save time, we save money. That's the business case. The rest is noise."

Olivia stayed still at the front of the room, hands relaxed at her sides.

"I hear you," she said calmly, "and I expected this reaction. Honestly, I'm glad you said it out loud.

"Let me be clear, however: we need to be smart. I'm not saying don't use technology. I'm saying use it thoughtfully. If you think ignoring the people side of this change will allow you to accelerate, wait until you see what turnover does to your service levels. Wait until your brand erodes because your bots are not servicing your customers. Wait until those who are too afraid to say anything just leave. Worse yet, wait until they stop caring because they are burned out. I have seen it happen before, and it is not pretty."

The room stayed still, tense, emotions brewing.

Richard stepped in, "We didn't bring Olivia in to permit us or to agree with everything you have already been doing. We included her to help us see what we've been missing."

He looked at Marcus. "We've tried your way, and we all know how that's worked out so far. Your Board brought us in to help fix this sinking ship. I am prepared to fight to the end to see if we can make this work. "

Marcus didn't respond. He didn't need to. The finances, the culture, and the employee disengagement told the story without words.

Richard then turned to the group. "We're not asking you to scrap anything you have already done. We're simply asking for your engagement on this journey. We are asking for a little grace and a willingness to step back, assess the situation, and help build something new and sustainable. Together."

Chapter Six
You Can't Lead What You Can't See

Marcus adjusted the cuff of his shirt as he stood looking out the window of his office. He had remodeled the space in stark contrast to how Richard had decorated it. He got rid of the mahogany bookshelves and replaced them with black metal shelves, decorated with abstract sculptures and crystal awards. The walls, once warm and wood-paneled, were now a matte slate gray with integrated lighting that illuminated his desk just enough to remind visitors who held the power in the room.

The desk itself was a large slab of glass and steel, placed purposefully so that Marcus always sat with his back to the view. Anyone seated across from him had to squint into the sunlight. All in an attempt to keep visitors off balance from the first handshake. Two leather chairs for guests sat a few inches lower than necessary. Everything in the room formed an intentionally crafted image that Marcus had spent years creating.

He glanced at the clock that hung on the far wall: five minutes until his weekly call with Nate and Dane. As he waited, Marcus rested his head against his chair, letting his mind wander a bit.

This company was different, as was this team, even though he had handpicked most of them. This... mess; he hadn't seen it coming.

His frustration could be seen on his face if anyone were in the room. His usual playbook wasn't working. Everything that had worked before- cost cuts, restructuring, and aggressive growth strategies- bounced off the walls of this place. Then, the ultimate insult, Silvergate bringing back the founders to fix what he couldn't.

The buzz of his phone snapped him out of his spiraling thoughts and developing migraine.

"Marcus," came Nate's voice. "How's it going with Richard and Alex?"

Marcus exhaled slowly, got up, and started pacing behind his desk. "It's a waste of time," he muttered. "They're stuck in a fantasy, talking about AI like it's a decision maker. They are treating our tools and systems like, well, like coworkers. I think it's crazy."

There was a pause. Then Dane cut in, his tone was sharp, "Do you have a better solution?"

Marcus's shoulders shot back, his posture suddenly rigid, while the silence hung in the air.

"No," he admitted, the proud edge in his voice dulled by fatigue. "This company's a dog with fleas. We should cut our losses before it tanks completely."

Dane's voice came through again, "That's not going to happen. We have too much invested in here. You'd better get on board and find a way to turn this around, or we'll find someone who can."

Marcus's jaw clenched as the other line went dead. There's no way in hell this company will ruin my reputation, he thought, and there's no way Richard and Alex will turn it around, not on my watch.

Richard, Alex, and Olivia sat at a corner table in her hotel. They usually met early for breakfast when she was in town. Today, they met to debrief on the workshop from the day before.

"Yesterday went as expected," Olivia said, stirring her tea. "We laid out the Talent Trek 2.0 framework, and they aren't buying it. Some, like David, are intrigued. But the others, well, Marcus and Emily couldn't hide their skepticism."

Richard laughed, "You call that hostility to the trek skepticism? We knew this wouldn't be easy. However, I can now see that we have an uphill battle in convincing Marcus that this is best for his company, and the team will have to make space to work through their challenges."

"Which is why, today," Olivia said, pulling out her notes, "we're breaking into smaller groups. People are more open when they aren't performing in front of a crowd. I want to get Brianne and Julie alone. IT and HR have to be in lockstep if we have any hope of integrating AI into workflows effectively."

"That makes sense," Alex said. "It seems like Brianne respects the technical challenge, but I think she's still viewing this simply from a systems lens."

Olivia responded, "Right, and we need the human systems– HR, culture, and training– all aligned with the digital infrastructure. Otherwise, we're setting this up to fail."

They reviewed the breakout assignments. Olivia would take Brianne and Julie. Richard would sit with Marcus and Emily. Alex would guide David and Carlos through their operational concerns.

Richard leaned his left elbow on the table and scrunched his nose, sighing, "I'll handle Marcus, but I'm not going to argue with him. I want to listen, really listen. It will not benefit the company if he isn't on board. I think I will use more of a Socratic method of asking questions."

"What does that look like?" Olivia asked.

"Like, his playbook's not working? Why does he think the same levers are failing now, when they worked in the past?"

Alex smiled. "This might be the first time someone holds up a mirror to him in a while."

"He won't like it," Richard added, "and hopefully he responds well."

Olivia glanced at her watch. "Time to get to it."

Olivia stood at the front of the boardroom, light from the window brightening the room. As the last of the team settled into their seats, she gave a glance to Richard and Alex, who nodded in return. The room quieted.

"Good morning, everyone," Olivia began. "Thank you for being here, and being open to what might be a different kind of session."

"Today, we will begin to rethink how we work. Before we dive into our leadership workshop, 'Rethinking the Workforce,' we'll start with something less formal but arguably more important: conversation. We want to have honest conversations in smaller breakout groups."

"I'll be spending time with Brianne and Julie," she continued, "because the alignment between IT and HR is going to be critical if we're serious about workforce transformation."

Brianne looked on, but Julie crossed her arms.

Olivia continued, "Richard will be with Marcus and Emily. Alex, you'll take David and Carlos."

There were a few sideways glances, but no objections, just a murmur of chairs shifting.

"Each of you has concerns, and that's valid," Olivia said, walking to prop the door open, "but we're asking that you bring those forward. We need to get everything on the table if we are to move forward."

The three women moved to a small conference room with just three chairs, a whiteboard, and a fresh carafe of coffee. Olivia had intentionally removed the power dynamics from the space. She wanted it to be a space that would promote a conversation.

Brianne entered first, saying, "No slides?"

"Nope," Olivia said with a smile. "We're just going to talk."

Julie followed, settling in beside her. "What do you want to talk about?"

"If this workforce transformation is going to work," Olivia said, "it starts with the two of you, and how IT and HR decide to work together."

Brianne had a questioning look on her face. "I don't understand. It sounds like you're trying to put lipstick on the pig. Dress up HR so it sounds cool or value-added." Julie gave Brianne a sideways glare that Brianne either did not see or chose to ignore.

Olivia took note of the animosity toward HR. She understood that the old stereotype was hard for some leaders to overcome.

"I would say, historically, you're not wrong. Most AI

initiatives have lived squarely inside IT, but that's the point. We've been treating AI as a system rather than something that is actually doing employee work."

Julie jumped in, "I'm confused. What do you mean?"

"We start by creating job descriptions for the AI tools," Olivia said, smiling. "We need to define what each AI system is responsible for, how it interfaces with human teams, what success looks like, where the handoffs happen, and who manages all of it.

"I want to integrate it like a co-worker, because whether we like it or not, employees already rely on the bots and AI agents. If an employee defers or blames the AI tool, then that is more than software. It becomes a workforce behavior that drives everything. Over time, it undermines the culture, significantly."

Julie leaned back, thinking aloud, "We can't just rebrand tools as team members. If we humanize AI too much, well, I just think of the Terminator movies."

"That's exactly why HR has to be at the table," Olivia said emphatically. "The way we talk about AI, and how we introduce it, is critical to successful change adoption. We must build the right connection with the new teammates, even though it's technology. If we can do that, it becomes ingrained into the culture, and the business will accelerate from there."

Brianne crossed her arms. "Let's say I buy that, which is a big 'if.' What does this type of integration look like? We've implemented a dozen systems and have a dozen more use cases we're working on. Are you saying we stop everything and do some company-wide AI offsite?"

Olivia chuckled, "No, but we should begin to establish a new level of workforce thinking into every AI use case going forward. Every time a new tool goes in, we need to ask ourselves, who will interact with it? What behaviors do we want to encourage? What are the risks of misuse? And who governs the decisions it makes? It's time to think about workforce architecture as part of the overall system architecture."

Julie nodded slowly. "Sounds like you are suggesting a governance model."

"Not entirely," Olivia said. "Governance will play a part in AI oversight strategy. At this point, I am looking at how HR can bring a perspective around employee enablement, learning, performance, and behaviors to values. IT brings the system infrastructure, security, and data governance. Together, you create a secure working environment where everyone succeeds."

Brianne uncrossed her arms and tapped her foot a few times before responding, "You know what concerns me most? Velocity. We are rolling these tools out faster than ever, and we need to. If we slow things down, we could fall behind our competitors and lose even more market share."

"Let me ask you, how many of your AI tools have been slow to adopt, are not being used, or are not capturing the ROI you expected?" Olivia replied.

There was silence from both women.

"Perhaps it is time to slow down, as we all know that sometimes going a bit slower on projects will accelerate the ultimate adoption and actually capture the expected ROI."

Julie asked, "This sounds like a lot of work. Where do we begin?"

"Today, we document the current scenarios," Olivia said. "We'll identify everywhere that AI's been implemented. We'll then surface any confusion or resistance among employees. After that, we can build a cross-functional map of the human-machine relationship across departments."

Alex's breakout was in a small conference room off the main hallway. It had a window with natural light, but otherwise was a standard meeting room. He figured he would have the easiest time of the three breakouts. David and Carlos arrived together, coffees in hand, and both appeared ready to engage in the conversation.

Alex made a gesture to have them take a seat and said, "This session's meant to be an open conversation. No BS, just an honest check-in to how you and your team are doing."

David shrugged. "That's good, because I'll be honest, I don't know what you expect from us. We're not against any of this, but we're not sure what to do with it either. The new Talent Trek has baffled me. The original trek was clear, and I am a big fan of it, but this one… I'm not sure what to make of it."

Carlos agreed, "I'm a big fan of AI, especially in sales and marketing, and we are already seeing some positive gains with the tool usage. Though, to be honest, there are parts that seem like we're stumbling in the dark as we navigate this new technology."

Alex agreed, "You're not alone in feeling that way. Many leaders find themselves in the same position. You see the promise of what AI could do, but don't have the time to think about how best to use it, or, for that matter, implement it."

David leaned forward. "I get that AI will bring value to the business. We just haven't seen much of it yet. We've got metrics to hit, and the financial pressures keep pushing us to absorb more costs. I have no idea why we aren't seeing the promised benefits yet."

"That's where I want to focus," Alex replied. "Olivia will be walking us through the process of embedding AI into the way your teams already work."

"I am not sure I understand," Carlos said, tilting his head.

Alex said, "Imagine an AI tool that flags anomalies in production efficiency and alerts the shift supervisor that something is going on. They can then decide on the best course of action."

"Sure, that sounds good, but I don't have extra resources to assign to an AI initiative," David responded.

"I am no expert, but my understanding is you don't need a full-blown AI team; instead, you need to make it part of your workforce strategy, as well as your systems implementation. It's something Olivia will walk us through in another session."

Carlos frowned. "It's a nice model, in theory. I've seen too many projects fail because we didn't plan properly. Oh, and let's not forget the change management aspect of implementing new technology. We definitely have been doing that lately."

Alex agreed, "We need to do things differently this time. Instead of starting with the tech and figuring out how to use it, we start with the technology's intention. We need to identify where your teams are losing time, figure out which decisions could be made faster, and understand what data we need to deliver it all. Then we will conduct a small-scale implementation and measure the impact. I think it will be important to make sure the right people are involved so we can get the most out of the tools."

David leaned back in his chair. "This isn't about replacing anyone."

"No," Alex said firmly. "You should know Richard and me long enough to know we would never be on board for a wholesale head-cutting exercise. Our goal is to keep your team focused on the high-value work and let AI handle the routine work, the analysis, and the non-value-added repetitive tasks."

Carlos exchanged a glance with David. "That's a start."

David replied, "It's worth a shot. I've seen what you and Richard have accomplished, so you have my trust on this one. Even though it is unorthodox."

"I'll take that as a win," Alex said. "Let's keep the conversation going. We still have a lot to talk about."

The room felt ten degrees colder than the others, which may have just been the ice-cold glares Richard was getting from Marcus.

Marcus sat at one end of the small round table, arms folded, his jaw moving as he clenched his teeth. Emily sat opposite him, her eyes were distant and unfocused as she stared out the window. Richard sat between them as a peer, in an attempt to foster an open dialogue and encourage Marcus to participate in the activity.

No one spoke at first.

Finally, Richard sighed and broke the silence, "I would like to talk openly and honestly about what you believe is happening at the company. What do you think is not working? Why do you think the company is struggling?"

Marcus snorted, "I see you're finally admitting that something's broken."

Richard didn't bite. "I see things aren't working. I just don't think we agree on what that something is."

Marcus leaned forward. "What's not working is this whole charade. All this talk about systems being part of the workforce. Frameworks named after treks. It's just a new name for corporate self-help. You know, I was a management consultant before being a CEO. I know all of the tricks."

Emily let out a shaky, uncomfortable breath.

"You've led turnarounds before, Marcus," Richard said. "I respect that. You have a playbook that's worked. Tell me, why isn't it working here?"

Marcus bristled, eyes narrowing. "Because this place isn't normal. You built a company where no one has to make hard decisions. Everyone's empowered, but no one's accountable. You over-emphasized culture, and now you've got people who care more about values than results."

He pointed directly at Richard now. "You built this mess."

"You do realize I have been gone for over five years, don't you? Yes, I built it, and at the time it worked. It attracted the top talent we needed to outperform larger, better-funded competitors. I now see that it was incomplete."

Emily raised an eyebrow. "Incomplete how?"

"I believed that if we hired the right people, gave them the right tools, and supported them, the rest would follow," Richard said. "It did, until the world changed. Actually, I think the world changed faster than anyone expected. We now have a trifecta impacting the employee base—AI, remote work, and changing values. Suddenly, people are now choosing meaning over jobs. The old model, yours and mine, is not enough."

"Now what? We just throw out everything that worked for decades?" Marcus spewed.

"No, I don't think that is the answer," Richard said. "We need to evolve it. Do you remember when e-commerce was going to kill brick-and-mortar shops? That was all that the consultants and the news pushed for a year. When reality kicked in, every organization had to evolve to change the business model to include the internet."

Emily resumed her disengaged stare out the window, and Marcus looked toward the door.

"Let me ask you something," Richard said, turning his focus directly on Marcus. "If I am correct, your standard playbook focuses on cost-cutting, aggressive restructuring, and rigorous performance metrics. Those strategies worked great for you in the past. Why do you think they're not working now?"

Marcus just looked at Richard.

Richard pressed gently, "I'm asking sincerely. I have seen that model work wonders, and want to hear what you see now that you are in the midst of this change."

Marcus stared at the table. "This… this workforce doesn't respond the same way. They question everything. They expect to have a voice in the change. They want the context before doing anything. They want to collaborate on everything before committing to the cause. It slows everything down."

Richard nodded. "Yes, it does."

"It's not scalable!" Marcus snapped. "I don't need a company full of toddlers asking 'why, why, why' and needing their hands held all along the way. I am running a company, not a daycare."

"Unfortunately, execution doesn't come from blind obedience anymore," Richard said quietly. "It comes from the engagement of the employees. People don't follow leaders because they fear them. They follow leaders they trust, and that trust has to be earned differently now."

Emily finally spoke again, "Where does AI fit into this? Isn't this supposed to be about transformation?"

"Yes," Richard said. "I think we have to lead this kind of transformation differently than we could in the past. Everything I know says it requires a mindset shift. Think of it this way: treating AI like any other system implementation reduces it to a cost-cutting tool, putting everyone on notice that their job is on the chopping block.

"However, treating it like an employee allows our real employees to relax a little and focus on being more productive. That simple distinction shapes how we go about implementation. It has broad-reaching implications on training, structure, culture, and trust in leadership."

Marcus exhaled, "You want me to rewrite my playbook based on what, emotions? Narratives? What's next, circle sharing time?" Marcus scoffed, shaking his head.

"I want you to expand it. Keep the rigor and accountability, but make room for something new. These new tools require greater flexibility and open minds to capture their real value. It's simply a new way to adapt to the business, Marcus."

Marcus looked up, a man bitter and defeated, but not foolish. "You really think this matters? Does treating AI like a co-worker change anything?"

"I think we are all on a journey of learning. With the changes in technology and capability, we must understand how work really happens—through people, processes, and now, systems. I'm not sure this is the final solution. In fact, I would guess it's not. But it is something that we should try. I also know we are not in Kansas anymore," Richard said, closing the meeting.

The room grew still as Marcus thought it through.

After the breakout sessions, they all took a well-deserved break. The coffee shop was a short walk around the corner from the office, a quiet refuge before the next round of workshops. Marcus ordered a cappuccino. Emily ordered a chai latte and found a small table near the window.

Emily spoke first, "Well, that meeting was unexpected."

Marcus sneered, "What? The part he tried to get us to sing Kumbaya?"

Emily chuckled softly. "No, I mean the part where he wanted to listen. I appreciated the fact that he didn't try to convert us through preaching. He tried to understand where our heads were at."

Marcus spat back, "He used that approach because he wants everyone to think that he was some sort of visionary instead of a leader who built a soft organization that is living in the past."

"Maybe," Emily said. "Or maybe he's just trying to course-correct. People can change, you know."

"Leaders don't," Marcus snapped. "Not really. They just learn to market their failures as pivots."

Emily watched him for a moment. "You're not wrong. This place needs a healthy dose of discipline. It also needs something else. I'm not even sure what that is, or what they're really proposing, yet. However, I know what we're doing isn't working."

"You think holding hands with a computer is going to fix that?"

"I think ignoring the shift in how people work and what they expect isn't going to fix it," she replied. "Look, I'm not all-in, but I'm not shutting the door just because the language feels new."

Marcus looked away as he felt a migraine coming on. "I took this job because I wanted to take this organization to the next level of performance. I run things my way, and if Silvergate wants a puppet, they can find someone else. I'm not running a daycare for underperforming managers and disenfranchised bots."

Emily shook her head. Voice lowered, she said, "You know what scares me more than change? Leaders who refuse to see it coming."

Marcus's head turned toward her with a daring glare. He stood abruptly and tossed his empty cup in the trash, heading for the door. "Let them come for my job if they want. At least I'll go down leading like a CEO, not a camp counselor."

Emily stayed seated, sipping her chai as Marcus walked off. She didn't know exactly where this was going, but she was open to seeing the possibility. She knew she would have to choose between Marcus and Richard. She didn't relish the idea of making that decision.

Returning from lunch, the elevator doors opened. Richard stepped out and looked around the newly reconfigured headquarters. It was quiet.

Everyone wore noise-canceling headphones. Dashboards lit up like Christmas trees. A few younger team members typed furiously, toggling between Slack threads and what appeared to be prompts using generative AI.

He walked past one pod and overheard a snippet:

"I don't want to bug her again. The system flagged it as complete, but I haven't seen the output."

Richard kept walking.

A few aisles later, Nina saw Richard and smiled. She was the first familiar face Richard saw besides David.

"Richard, it's been a long time. I heard you were wandering the halls," she said as he approached.

"Nina, it is great to see you. How are you?"

"I am okay. It's not the same company that you left, but you probably already know that."

"That's why I'm here: to see what's going on," Richard said. "How is engagement? How are the rest of the employees doing?"

"Disengaged," Nina said hesitantly.

"Really? Help me understand what's going on," Richard asked her to explain.

Nina then gave him an example of how her team had missed a deadline. Not by much, just a day, but enough to rattle a client. She tried to tighten oversight and implemented daily status checks and reporting updates. She looked to AI for more information than her employees could provide.

"And?"

"As I said, they're disengaging," she said. "Quietly, but it's there. They do what I ask, but the spark's gone. Marcus is driving us to deliver, so we do, but no one is happy about the way they are required to execute."

Richard looked at her with empathy. "What are you hoping they'll do?" He asked.

Nina didn't hesitate. "I don't know. Take some ownership, think like the leaders they are, and help flag issues before they break. Unfortunately, most are now just focused on doing the task and going home."

"What do they need from you to do that?"

Nina paused. "Probably not more spreadsheets," she said with a defeated laugh.

Richard was surprised by Nina's comments but began to see what had happened to his company.

Chapter Seven
Redrawing the Work

The clouds had been gathering all afternoon. It was the kind of sky that made it hard to tell whether a storm was passing or about to arrive. Richard noticed it as he took his seat and thought how fitting it felt.

He and Alex hadn't spoken much since lunch.

Richard's brief hallway exchange with Nina hit him harder than expected. She hadn't complained or blamed leadership. She'd simply sounded done. Her defeated tone was full of sadness, as if she had once loved her job and had put her life into it. As Richard thought about her, he would have understood her to be burned out or angry, but her detachment from the company and the team she was responsible for was shocking. It was almost as if she'd made peace with leaving without ever saying so. He had heard about the concept of quiet quitting, but had never seen it in person. Now he had, and it suddenly had a face: Nina.

Quiet quitting, Richard realized, was a look in someone's eyes. He started wondering, who else has that look here?

Marcus entered the room with the same irritated expression he had throughout the morning. Emily followed a few minutes later, which was unusual since she was usually only a step behind her boss. When she got to her chair, she didn't sit down immediately. She leaned on the back of the chair, eyes looking at something across the room. The rest of the team filtered in behind her, noticing the slight shift in her posture. Whatever the breakout sessions had stirred up, it hadn't drained them. If anything, it had heightened their curiosity.

Olivia waited until the room settled.

"Welcome back. I hope you had a good lunch and a chance to catch up on emails. This afternoon, we move to step one of the Talent Trek 2.0. We're going to do something most companies skip entirely. We're going to map the truth."

A few brows lifted and heads cocked to the side.

"We talk a lot about talent strategy," she continued, "but how often do we actually look at the work itself? Who does what? Which processes are being powered by people, partners, or machines? What have we outsourced? Automated? Augmented? Let's get all of that on the wall."

She turned and tapped the wall behind her. Beside her hand, five oversized poster boards stretched across the wall, each marked with clean horizontal swim lanes. They were titled: Operations, Finance, HR, Sales & Marketing, and IT. In the middle of the conference room table sat stacks of sticky notes in three distinct colors.

"Before we talk about strategy," Olivia said calmly, "we need to understand the current state."

She paused.

"Most companies skip this part. We talk about talent in terms of roles and headcount, but we rarely look at the work itself. Not who's accountable, but who's actually doing it?"

She gestured to the wall. "This afternoon is about mapping the truth of your current workforce."

There was a subtle shift in the room. Chairs straightened. Pens came out. People leaned in without realizing it.

"Many of you are underestimating your W3 footprint. Why? Because we see tools as support, not staff. In the age of agentic AI, that's outdated thinking. These systems are both assisting and acting, and that makes them part of your workforce.

"I know what you are thinking. Why does this matter?" Olivia let the silence hang for a moment. "Here's the truth. If you don't know who's doing the work, you can't lead it effectively. You can't optimize it, and you certainly can't scale it."

She pointed to the wall of swim lanes. "What you're about to uncover is your workforce composition. Most companies think they're ninety percent W1, with a little outsourcing sprinkled in, but when you do this honestly, the numbers look very different, and that shift changes everything: how you hire, train, build culture, and lead," she said, looking at Marcus.

Olivia took a few slow steps forward and then began again, "Each of you has a set of three color-coded sticky notes. We will get to the definition shortly, but know that each color represents W1, W2, and W3."

A few executives reached for one pad of each color and inspected the palette.

"I know you've all seen org charts and project trackers, RACI matrices, and SOPs. Today, we're not mapping the organizational hierarchy, we're mapping how and where the work actually gets done," Olivia emphasized the last statement. She paused, making eye contact with each person.

"This is the first step of the Talent Trek 2.0: clarify the workforce landscape. It's the foundation for everything we'll build in the days ahead. You can't lead a workforce you don't fully see.

"Each of you has forty-five minutes. Pick one real process, don't overthink it. Break it down into distinct actions. For each one, write it on a sticky note and label it clearly. Just map a single process from your function," Olivia continued. "Not the whole org chart, not your ideal state, just one real process. Something your team performs regularly. Step by step, write out each activity on a separate sticky note and color-code it based on who actually does the work.

"For each step, you will answer three questions:

- Who, physically or digitally, completes the task?
- What tools or systems are involved?
- If that person or system disappeared tomorrow, what would break?

"Here's the key, don't think about who's accountable. Rather, think about who performs the action."

Olivia looked around to ensure everyone was with her and then passed out a sheet of paper.

"To have some consistency, when you label the workforce responsible for a task, use the green sticky for your W1, which includes your full-time or part-time employees on your payroll. A good example might be a supply chain analyst who runs demand planning each Monday.

"The blue sticky will be your W2 workforce, who are your contractors, consultants, third-party providers, or gig talent. Julie, this is where your PEO partner that handles benefits administration would come into play.

"Finally, the yellow sticky is your W3 workforce, which includes your AI agents, bots, algorithms, and intelligent systems performing tasks autonomously or semi-autonomously. Think about an RPA bot that reconciles invoices or an AI tool that scans social media to gather necessary customer data.

"When time is up, you'll go to the wall and place each sticky note into your swim lane that matches your function. And then," Olivia smiled, "we're going to walk the wall together. You'll each explain your process, one by one. What you'll begin to see, probably for the first time, is the true shape of your workforce."

Olivia took a breath and gave one final piece of information, "You can't lead a W3 workforce with a W1 mindset. Any questions?"

Julie spoke up, "If an AI tool screens resumes, that's W3? Even the bots?"

"Especially the bots," Olivia said, glad that the team seemed to understand the exercise. "If a vendor performs background checks, that is a blue sticky. Of course, if your recruiter sends the offer letter, that is green."

"What if a person and a system are both involved in the task?" Carlos asked.

"Good question. In that case, write both. If there's a handoff, split the sticky note or stack them. We want to see the interaction, which may be an ideal place to overlay a governance step."

With all questions answered, the group got to work. For the next forty-five minutes, the room was largely quiet except for the sound of sticky notes being scribbled and peeled. Executives moved between their laptops, texting a few team members to confirm which software handled which tasks.

Marcus spent his time answering emails and working on his next board deck. He was required to be there, but not to pay attention or participate. He continued to feel that this activity was a waste of time for him and his team. They had better things to do than to play around with sticky notes, he thought, and the more he thought about it, the angrier he got. Finally, he couldn't take it any longer. He closed his laptop, got up, and left the room without saying anything.

Everyone in the room looked up, wide-eyed and casting looks around the room to figure out what was going on. David shrugged his shoulders and got back to work. Soon, the rest of the staff followed suit. They were all engaged in making the most of this exercise, even if they weren't one-hundred percent sold.

"Do we count the chatbot that answers customer FAQs?" Carlos looked up and asked Olivia.

"If it solves problems on its own," she replied, "then yes, put it on a W3 sticky."

"Damn," he said, switching a green note to yellow.

Carlos leaned over to David and whispered, "I feel like I should've brought a second set of hands for all this funnel data."

David chuckled. "Just don't make us look bad with some color-coded marketing magic."

When Olivia called time, each executive stood in turn and walked to the wall.

"Alright," she said, "let's see your real workforce in action. Let's take this one at a time. Grab your notes and head to the wall."

Julie stood, and the entire stack slipped from her hand, falling to the floor.

"Oh no, sticky note clean up on aisle three," Carlos said with a laugh.

"Classic HR making a mess of things," Brianne added with a grin.

Julie rolled her eyes with mock exasperation as she bent over to gather the notes. "When will a bot be able to clean up my mess?" she said.

The room chuckled, the tension melting just a little.

"Need a W3 assistant for that?" Richard said from the back.

"I'd settle for a W2 intern," Julie replied as she walked to the board to place her sticky notes.

Her recruiting process unfolded visually, one task at a time, until the pattern became impossible to ignore. Resume screening.

Offer letters. Welcome emails. Automated onboarding steps. The yellow notes clustered faster than anyone expected.

Julie stepped back, arms crossed, studying her own lane. "We used to touch every part of this," she said quietly. "Now we mostly oversee it."

Julie could answer most of the questions thrown at her, but a few caught her off guard and made her think a little longer than she would have liked. Questions like, "At what point in this process does a human actually make a decision, and are we comfortable with where that line currently sits?" and "How do we know the system is making the same choices we would make today, not the choices we made two years ago when we configured it?"

Julie opened her mouth, paused, then said, in almost a confession, "I don't have great answers for those questions. It has been an aha moment for me right now. This activity has uncovered some real gaps in my understanding."

Olivia let the comment sink in with the group, then nodded once. "Don't look at this as a failure. Take it as an opportunity to learn and lead.

"Most executives believe leadership comes from having all of the answers," Olivia continued. "In reality, it comes from asking the right questions, and from being willing to admit when the system has outpaced our understanding."

She gestured back toward Julie's swim lane. "Nothing on that wall is wrong, but some of it was invisible. You can't govern what you haven't acknowledged."

Olivia stepped back, deliberately returning the attention to the group. "This exercise is trying to uncover where our blind spots are so we can see them clearly enough to get them fixed."

She then added, "The most dangerous workforce decisions are the ones we don't realize we've already delegated. Good job, Julie, and thank you for your courage to lead the way."

Emily followed with the quarterly close process. Surprisingly, a third of her flow was marked W3, with auto-reconciling tools and variance analyzers.

Grabbing his stack, Carlos moved to his swim lane. "Let's see what the magic eight ball has to say," he joked. "I decided to take a look at my demand generation funnel from lead gen to deal closure."

He continued to explain how marketing automation had gradually taken over their campaign sequencing. "It started with scheduling," he said. "Now, it's also generating headlines, adjusting audience targets, and even tweaking the creative mid-flight. Most of the campaign flow doesn't touch a human until it's reporting." He placed sticky note after sticky note as he talked.

He took a step back. "I knew we had automation," he admitted, scanning the mostly yellow swim lane, "but this is beyond what I thought."

"Wait," said David, eyeing Carlos's board. "You have bots writing proposals?"

"They pull from templates and past deals. You would be amazed at how much time it saves us, but we still do the negotiating."

David was next to step forward, meticulously placing his sticky notes on his swim lane. Everyone remarked how neat his writing was. It was readable, even from the other side of the room.

He turned and looked back at the group. "I guess we have more bots than bodies," he said.

Finally, Brianne approached the IT swim lane. Despite her earlier grumbling, she'd clearly done the work. "I decided to look at my help-desk and customer service process."

She described how their IT ticketing system used an AI triage assistant to route seventy percent of tickets, more than she realized. "And when she can't fix it, she escalates to our offshore W2 team," Brianne said. "Honestly, I didn't even think of that assistant as part of the workforce. Oh, and I didn't include that we also use AI to analyze the data. She's better at recognizing patterns than most junior analysts."

"She?" asked Carlos.

"I guess I just think of our chatbot as a girl. We used to worry about shadow IT; turns out the real shadows are digital teammates we never acknowledged."

Once everyone had finished placing their sticky notes onto the swim lanes, a tapestry emerged in all three colors.

"This is your actual workforce," Olivia said quietly, purposefully sweeping her arm out to the side, "This is the landscape you built."

Yellow was everywhere, and it shocked everyone in the

room. No one expected as much W3 usage as they had.

Carlos stopped staring at the wall and asked, "If this represents just one workflow for each of our functions, what does that mean about the rest of them?"

Brianne chimed in, "Crap, I had no idea we had implemented so much AI into the system. If I am not aware, then it may be more pervasive than any of us think."

"Which may be why morale and engagement have plummeted and why employees are concerned for their jobs," Julie said.

"What you're feeling right now is common," Olivia said. "Every executive team I run this with has the same reaction. Surprise. Concern. And then the instinct to either celebrate the efficiency or blame the technology. The real issue isn't how much W3 you're using, it's how *unacknowledged* it is."

She tapped one of the yellow notes. "These systems are doing real work. Making real decisions. Affecting real people, yet most of your employees have never heard leadership talk about them as part of the workforce."

Olivia explained that, just as nature abhors a vacuum, so does an organization. When a gap opens up, employees often step in. Management generally has no idea that employees are filling the gaps. If that is the case, where a manager is clueless, you begin to see trust erode and morale drop. Managers must know what is happening on the ground. When you throw in AI, employees suddenly worry about their jobs. All of these factors create anxiety, and systemic anxiety in an organization is a recipe for failure.

After her teaching, Olivia stepped back, giving the wall one last look. "You didn't do anything wrong by adopting W3. You are responsible for integrating it. Your task is to create clarity, visibility, and openness by creating a shared story about AI, where the organization is going with the technology and how the employees need to partner with it."

A few heads nodded.

"When there's no shared story," Olivia said, "people write their own. We should be the ones who fill in the gaps of the stories through better communication. If we begin with governance, redesign, or optimization, you will face an employee base that is making up their own narrative.

"W3 must be a relationship shift, now that you have a workforce that consists of humans, contractors, and autonomous systems. That means you need to manage work across all three groups."

She gestured to the poster wall. "Right now, you can see the flow of tasks; however, the next phase is about designing the system. Who owns the work? Who makes the decisions? Where do relationships need to be reinforced?

"I am going to give you some homework for tomorrow," she said, handing out a worksheet titled **Workforce Role Debrief**. The paper contained four key questions that each leader needed to answer:

- What surprised you?
- Where is W3 leading instead of assisting?
- Where is W2 critical but invisible?
- What relationships are missing?

"We're going to close today with one more layer," Olivia said, "'Return on Relationship' or 'RoR' for short.

"Every team needs to understand what part they play and who is in the game with them. When the relational interaction is blocked, we see performance tanking, even when everything looks 'automated.' The teams that thrive with W3 are the ones with the strongest human-to-human relationships."

She walked over and opened one more folder. Pulling out more sheets of paper, she handed one out to each participant. At the top of the page were the words, *The Relational Role Audit*.

"Our next task is to understand the human connections. We'll use this activity to explore who influences whom, what rituals maintain trust among employees, and which relationships are strategic, not just structural.

"Tomorrow," Olivia said, "we'll begin building your new blueprint. For now, look at the wall. Here is your company. This is your real workforce."

No one responded because, for the first time, the staff began to see what Olivia had been talking about for two days.

The restaurant was quiet, tucked away in a charming part of town.

Kathy loved its worn wood floors, crooked tables, and string lights that made everything feel just a little softer.

Richard set his half-empty glass of wine down and looked at his wife. "Today felt," he paused, "like the team started to be honest with themselves and about the company for the first time."

Kathy sipped her wine. "It sounds like you've had some good progress with the workshop."

"Yes, though I am a bit humbled about the changes in the workforce. I've spent decades thinking about work in terms of org charts, job descriptions, and annual reviews. Yet, today, I watched every executive realize how much of the real work is being done by people they don't see, and tools they don't understand."

She smiled gently. "You've always been good at looking under the surface."

He shook his head. "Not this time. Olivia's leading us through this process, and it's clear we've all been blind to what's truly driving our results. AI, external partners, and automated tools are all around us. Unfortunately, we've done a poor job integrating it with the human side."

He paused, swirling the last of his drink. There was a moment of quiet between them.

"I tried ChatGPT today," Kathy said, looking a bit embarrassed.

Richard raised an eyebrow. "Really?"

"Don't act so surprised," she grinned. "I had to write a thank-you message to a donor prospect, and I was completely stuck. Then I remembered that you told me it's a great tool to help me get started. Well, with writer's block, I was desperate enough to try. I typed in what I needed, and it gave me something to work with. What Chat spit out didn't sound like me at all, but it gave me enough to get going."

"And?"

"Well, I finally understand what you've been telling me—and don't even think about telling me 'I told you so!'"

He chuckled, "You've officially leveraged the Third Workforce."

She smiled. "Maybe, or maybe I just stopped resisting what could help me do more of what matters."

Richard sat back. "You know, that's the lesson I've been

thinking about all day."

"What is?"

"That maybe leadership is about knowing you don't have all of the answers and, more importantly, where you can go to get help. Whether from a person or a smart AI tool."

She reached across the table and took his hand. "That sounds like good leadership growth."

"It sounds like the beginning of a new world."

Kathy nodded. "Then it's a good day."

"It was," Richard said as he smiled at her.

"You know what Olivia said right before we wrapped up?" he added. "She said tomorrow will be about choosing what we want this company to become. By building an ecosystem where human relationships are strong, and systems are leveraged to augment the total workforce."

Kathy furrowed her brow. "That sounds like a tall order."

"Yeah, what's interesting is that I'm not dreading the weight of it. I'm kind of curious."

Kathy squeezed his hand again. "Then go be curious."

As the waiter brought the check, Richard pulled out his phone and made a quick note for the morning session.

Chapter Eight
What Actually Moves Work

The building was still quiet when Olivia arrived. She usually arrived early to prepare for the day's session. She set her coffee down and proceeded to pin a new poster to the wall beside yesterday's maps. At the top, it read, *The Future-State Blueprint.* Below it were three familiar rows— W1, W2, W3. Beneath them, she added a fourth layer, labeled 'Relationships.'

She stepped back and studied it for a moment. Yesterday had been about seeing reality. Today would be about deciding what kind of organization they intended to become. The executives filtered in with a different energy than the previous days. The surprise of discovering how widely used W3 already was in the organization had kept most of them thinking about it all night. They couldn't help but wonder how it happened and what they needed to do about it. One thing was for sure: each executive now had a better understanding of why the organization was struggling.

Julie and Carlos arrived first, whispering about the office coffee situation. Emily followed, walking straight to the wall reviewing yesterday's maps.

Finally, Marcus walked in and stood behind his chair, hands resting on the back, waiting for the rest of the executive team to filter in.

Once everyone had settled, Marcus cleared his throat and got everyone's attention. "I won't be joining you today. I've pressing business issues to attend to. Two customers have escalated issues to me, and I need to determine why our forecast has been off for three consecutive weeks. I gave this charade a chance, but yesterday felt like a lot of theater with little substance."

He glanced at Olivia and shifted his gaze to Richard.

"No offense intended, but I don't have the luxury of mapping out sticky notes about bots when we're missing our numbers. I won't stop any of you from staying, but I am not going to spend more time on this shit."

He quickly pivoted, grabbing the open door and pulling it closed behind him before anyone could respond.

No one rushed to fill the silence.

Olivia was not surprised. She half expected him to excuse himself, though she had hoped he would change his position on this strategic activity. She nodded to herself and said, "At a time like this, I remember something I heard once. You don't build the future by reacting to the present. Now is the time for anyone else to take their leave, should you also consider the work we are doing to be crap."

No one moved.

"Good," she said. "Next, we are going to be working on architecture. Today, we will focus on building the blueprint."

She looked around the room to a few nods. She waited a few seconds and then said, "Let's get to work."

She didn't dwell on Marcus's exit. Resistance, she knew, often stemmed from fear rooted in a loss of control. She was glad the rest of the executive team seemed on board with the workshop, as she was ready to start building something solid today.

Yesterday, they mapped the work, tasks, handoffs, systems, and the growing presence of W3. It highlighted to the team the extent of the enterprise's technology disruption. Today's session would focus on what happened between people, the informal conversations, and important connections between co-workers that were now uncommon or absent. It was easy to think about systems and processes, but the relationships were a key component that would provide insight faster than any dashboard.

"Every organization runs on three things," Olivia said. "Skills, systems, and social connection."

She briefly paused and then said, "Skills tell us what people can do. Systems tell us how work gets executed. The social layer, however, is who talks to whom, who trusts whom, and who knows when something's about to break; it's your nervous system."

It was like a lightbulb went off in the room. Not a single executive had considered how relationships across the organization played a vital part in the success. Each of them considered the relationships and social networks within the function. The fog began to lift and they started to see why many decisions stalled: insights arrived too late, and teams worked hard but never gained traction.

Olivia continued, "In the push for speed, we tend to design a formal structure that maximizes moving fast. Very few individuals even know about the informal roles, or just assume they will take care of themselves. When you added the other workforces into the structure, you unintentionally thinned the connective tissue. You might be delivering more tasks, but you're talking less, and that is having a significant impact on the business."

She turned back around and drew three concentric circles

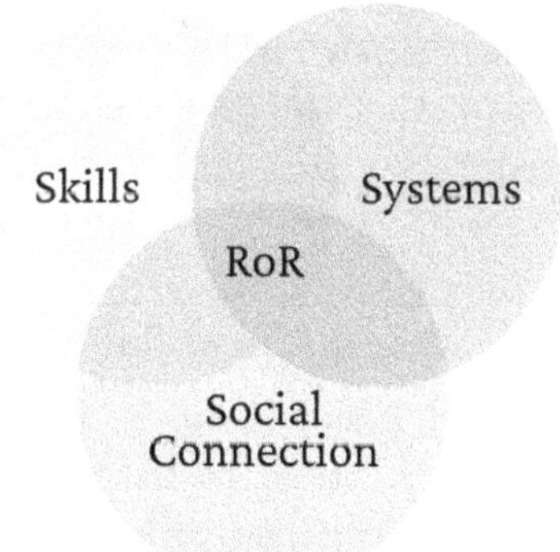

with skills, systems, and social connections.

"The skills, systems, and social connections of your employees make up the 'Return on Relationship,' which creates value through intentional human connection[1]. Think of it in terms of the influence of informal leaders or the flow of knowledge across silos. Right now, your Return on Relationship, or RoR, is low.

1 "Better People Analytics Measure who they know, not just who they are" by Paul Leonardi and Noshir Contractor

"We've spent the last day uncovering what work gets done and by which part of the workforce, but now we need to talk about how work moves through people, not just through systems and SOPs.

"The relational flow map is the connective tissue of your organization, and quite frankly, very few companies pay any attention to it. You've optimized for speed, technology, and reporting lines, but very few of you have optimized for trust, communication, and collaboration."

She paused long enough to let the message sink in. "Relationships," she continued, "are the invisible drivers of human performance. The stronger your relationships are, the more innovation and engagement you get. You also accelerate projects and decision-making. When they're weak, decisions get bottlenecks, blame becomes part of the culture, and work slows to a crawl."

Julie nodded silently. Emily scribbled something into her notebook. Even Richard leaned forward.

"As I said, this next layer is about identifying these roles within your function. Who plays them? Who used to? And, critically, who should be playing them as you grow? Here's what we're going to do," Olivia said, motioning toward five easel pads lining the walls of the room. "You'll work individually to map the relational landscape of one process from your function, the same one you did yesterday. But today, you'll layer in the people, not the tasks."

She handed out small color-coded sticky notes again and said, "Use pink to represent direct collaborators or people or roles you work with weekly or more. Use orange to indicate those you interact with occasionally, but who impact your success. Finally, use the purple sticky note to highlight people or roles you should be in a relationship with, but aren't."

Olivia continued, "You will be mapping your formal and informal networks. You must be honest with yourself. Also, be sure to focus on any handoff that feels stretched or nonexistent. Don't worry too much if you rely on a digital system. Though please mark that as well, as we'll discuss how W3 affects the human relationship network."

Julie purposefully dropped half her stack of notes on the

way up and laughed, "Well, I guess my relationships are falling apart already."

The room chuckled. Carlos quipped, "That's what happens when HR is too hands-off."

Everyone got to work on tracing the relationships across the organization. They began mapping who they relied on most, who influenced decision outcomes, who smoothed tensions between different functions, and who should be involved in key decisions or projects but weren't. Clear patterns began to emerge with gaps where communication failed and where collaboration was inconsistent. They could also see clusters of people where relationships and trust accelerated work and delivered better outcomes.

When they finished, they all stepped back to look at the wall. The clarity of the relational connection was startling to the team. Where the connections were strongest and weakest stood out like a neon sign. Finance and Sales were operating on parallel tracks. HR and IT barely spoke to each other despite having shared systems. Operations were relying largely on their own organization, with few relationships outside it.

Olivia moved to the back of the room to study the maps as a whole so she could see the patterns. She was looking for the blank spaces in between the notes. She pointed to the blank spaces on the wall and let the team know that was where people assumed someone else owned it, or where work slowed due to a lack of connections in the relational network. The result was that the right people were rarely included in the process, causing individuals to second-guess decisions or simply ignore the progress.

She moved her hand slowly across one empty stretch of paper. "Do you see this stretch here? It's an issue that is definitely impacting profitability and efficiency. If we dug into it deeper, we would see that there is a lot of rework, or the output is late, or in some cases, may be missed altogether."

Then, she had the team look at the purple stickies scattered across the maps. "Each one marks a handoff that didn't work for several reasons. Maybe it's a relationship that existed on paper but not in practice. Maybe there is a dependency that no one has formally acknowledged, therefore it is missed. These are the real gaps in ownership. It is not anyone's fault, but it has the same effect because the message gets lost or arrives too late. Unfortunately, this is also where decisions get made in isolation, forcing downstream teams to compensate."

She paused and said, "I know you have seen this. The Sales team promised something but didn't bother to ask Operations whether they could deliver it within the negotiated time frame. Orders become late, and the impact appears after the month or quarter close. Internally, we start pointing fingers, and it is the customers who get the short end of the stick."

Olivia was right; they had all lived some version of this kind of relational disconnect.

She explained, "In many companies, execution rarely fails because strategy is wrong. It usually fails because relationships don't carry information fast enough or far enough to keep the system aligned. In every organization, certain roles emerge whether leaders design them or not. Someone who knows how to pull the right people together when things get complicated. Someone who hears about a problem early and surfaces it to the right people. Someone who interprets functions, people, and systems and helps keep the work moving.

"When those roles are clear, the results start showing up, even when no one is looking. Work progresses efficiently, and issues get resolved before being escalated. In the end, teams seem to move faster. When relationships are missing, you need more meetings, more follow-ups, and a whole lot of wasted energy to get the work done.

"Relational capital is as tangible as any financial metric," Olivia continued. "In the age of AI and a heavily distributed workforce, your competitive advantage is your talent and how well they connect within the organization, which is why I am not a fan of a full remote workforce, but that is a whole different topic."

Richard spoke up and asked, "Are you really saying that relationships are the glue that keeps everything moving?"

"That is a good way to put it, Richard," Olivia said, nodding. "Which is why we moved from workforce maps to relational maps."

A few confused glances passed around the table.

Julie said hesitantly, "Would this look like an org chart of who likes each other?"

Olivia chuckled, "Not quite. We'll go over it in our next session."

Looking at her watch, Olivia decided to give everyone a break before moving to the next session. Once the Executive Assistant brought fresh coffee, the executives filed in and took their seats. Olivia stood in front of the wall of maps.

"Here's what we're doing next," Olivia began. "Each of you will map out a critical process from your function again, but this time, I want you to note who makes the work flow smoothly."

Olivia explained that each leader would review their relationship map and focus on weak and missing connections. In these purple and orange spaces, where collaboration was inconsistent or absent altogether, they would ask a harder question: who, today, is actually doing the work of connecting this system? And are they supposed to be?

"When relational gaps keep showing up," she continued, "it signals a role-design issue, as well as a lack of interaction between employees.

"In many cases, you'll find someone doing the tasks informally, on top of their day job, and in others, you'll find it slips through the cracks. Both are signals."

Passing out a worksheet[2], Olivia began to explain, "There are three informal roles that each person can play within an organization. These are roles people fall into because the system needs them to.

"The first is a 'Connector.' They bring people together across silos. They know who to call, who to loop in, and who's missing from the table. The second is the 'Signal Amplifier.' They surface issues or have insights that no one else sees before they become problems. These individuals are often the voice people listen to, even if they don't hold formal power. Finally, there is a 'Bridge Role.' They sit at the intersections between departments, tools, and even the corporate culture. They help translate and interpret, and ensure everyone is aligned."

Richard leaned back slightly, eyes still on the wall. He understood what he was seeing here intrinsically, though he never had a name for it. Now he felt he did.

"In every turnaround I've been part of," he said, "there were always a few people who had a level of influence that no organization chart could ever capture. You didn't realize it until they left the company and everything seemed to unravel."

2 See Appendix for reference

Olivia nodded. "Those people were playing relational roles, whether anyone asked them to or not."

Alex set his handout down and stepped closer to the maps, studying the purple gaps. His mind went somewhere else entirely.

"It looks like this is also where the biggest risks live," he said. "If no one owns those connections, then decisions depend on individuals, not systems. When individuals leave or get burned out, it becomes a single point of failure."

He tapped one of the empty spaces. "You really don't see this until it's too late. By then, the margin is already eroded, and the board is yelling at you."

Richard looked back at the function map he was standing in front of. "We've spent years rewarding people for execution, but we've been relying on relationships we never acknowledged, and never protected."

There seemed to be an awareness that this activity was turning an invisible, unappreciated task into a visible, acknowledged one. With that, Olivia decided it was time to begin the next exercise.

"Let's use the handout I gave you to add another layer to the function maps. You will find each core relational role listed, along with space to name who currently plays them, who should play them, and where ownership is entirely missing. Please take some time to fill out the chart for the function you have been mapping."

The team got to work and layered in the relational roles onto their maps. New patterns emerged as the color-coded stickies revealed the relational clusters and gaps—the gaps where the work stalled. Interestingly, there seemed to be a few people in certain roles who kept the whole company moving.

Alex studied the wall again and said, "I think we've been treating the delays, rework, and disengagement like isolated problems. Looking at these maps, however, explains a lot. I have a better appreciation as to why decisions and improvements don't always stick."

"I think we were putting Band-Aids on the symptoms," Richard added quietly.

Olivia agreed, "That is what most organizations do. However, by fixing the relational foundation, you can make sure the system works more smoothly."

As the team took their seats again, a realization overcame them. The work ahead hadn't gotten any easier, but it had gotten a lot clearer what they needed to do.

"When you focus on the infrastructure of relationships, you enable people to become a multiplier that helps with everything else you are attempting to do," Olivia summarized.

With everyone finally on board, they could move to the next step.

As the team moved out for lunch, Richard lingered behind. He looked at the maps again, taped up, colorful, chaotic, honest.

He leaned against the edge of the conference table, arms folded, watching as Olivia prepared for the next session. Alex stood nearby, flipping through his notebook, expression unreadable.

"Any chance Marcus changes his mind?" Richard asked bitterly.

Olivia didn't look up right away. She carefully pulled off the elastic band around a rolled chart. Finally, turning to face them both, she said, "He's not the villain here. He's overwhelmed. Probably afraid. Everything we're doing here threatens his playbook, the foundation of his career. How would you react if you were told the foundation you built your career on is no longer viable, and you would have to build something new?"

Richard was tired of Marcus' games. "His leadership hasn't delivered a win in over a year. He must see that it's insanity to keep trying something that's not working."

Olivia nodded. "I know, but it's worth remembering, resistance isn't always about arrogance. Sometimes, it's grief. People grieve the version of themselves they don't recognize anymore."

Alex looked up from his notes. "That's a fair point."

Richard let out a slow breath. "Fair or not, he's dragging this team down. I honestly don't care if he is open-minded or not. He has to be on board to lead this team through this transition."

There was a silence between the three of them. Not tense, just honest.

Alex sighed, "I'll call Nate. Not yet. Let's get through the blueprint work this afternoon, but after that, he needs to know Marcus isn't the one to lead this into the next phase."

Richard nodded, grateful for Alex putting their feelings into words. "No more wasted days. No more detours."

Olivia sighed, as well, and leaned against the table. She bit the inside of her cheek and took a moment to weigh the next steps before responding, "Then let's make this afternoon count, because what we're building needs every leader to be in alignment, and if they're not willing to walk forward, they shouldn't be blocking the path."

Chapter Nine
The Third Workforce

The sun broke through the clouds, clearing away all traces of the morning mist. The air felt lighter, and the whole team felt it. Even Emily, who had held on to her skepticism for most of the morning, returned from lunch with a changed posture. She didn't say anything right away, but she smiled when she entered.

Carlos was the first to speak as he took his seat, "Alright, let's build this thing."

Olivia grinned. "You read my mind."

She stood in front of the large room, filled with new materials. Over lunch, she had written, *Future State Workforce Blueprint* on the board.

Olivia began, "Before we jump in, let's do a quick recap. This morning, you mapped how the work gets done by employees, contractors, and W3. You mapped the relationships that keep things moving and identified who ensures the work gets done. You did a great job; it's not an easy task. "

She paused for a moment, scanning the wall full of posters with sticky notes, giving the team a moment to take in how much they accomplished in the morning session.

"Now, we move into building the organization we want to

have. This is where strategy meets aspiration. The blueprint you'll create this afternoon will examine tools, people, and processes. What work matters most? Who's best equipped to do it? And how do we create a workforce that's efficient and capable of delivering results?"

Emily, who had remained quiet for most of the morning, spoke, "I'm guessing this isn't a solo activity."

Olivia smiled. "Far from it. As you did this morning, each of you will lead one process redesign. Same swim lanes, but this time, we're starting with the future in mind."

She passed around a worksheet and framed the process they would use, which was similar to what they had already experienced. However, this time they would be working on a hypothetical structure that closed the gaps. They would describe how the process should or could work with the right structures, tools, and people.

Julie asked, "What if we don't know what tools we might need?"

"You won't have all the answers, and that's okay. The point of this activity is to design a model where the right work gets done by the right part of your workforce, and the right relationships are in place to keep it running smoothly."

The executives got to work.

As she did in the morning session, Julie focused on the recruiting process, reducing handoffs and utilizing a digital assistant to enhance the candidate experience. However, she made sure that every offer letter still came from a human.

"Some experiences," she said aloud, "should still come with a personal touch."

"What was that, Julie?" David asked.

"Just thinking out loud."

Emily rebuilt the quarter-close with fewer last-minute heroics and late-night work.

Across the room, Carlos traced the path of customer feedback and realized how often it got lost in a black box. He decided to add a step requiring a person to review it and engage with the customer when necessary.

David's focus was on the incessant rework that kept some machines busy. When timelines were tight, this process misbehaved and required valuable time to fix the problem– a Band-Aid, to be more precise. He designed the process to ensure fewer changeovers, handoffs, and variability.

Brianne, however, thought less about uptime and more about comfort with the tools. Automation handled the volume just fine; however, she now knew it required people to handle the judgment piece. Not having at least one person involved in a process, she decided, was no longer acceptable for what she wanted to accomplish.

When it was clear all of the executives had finished, Olivia said, "Now step back and tell me what you see."

There was a pause as people looked at their notes.

Then Richard said it first, "This new future state seems more balanced between human and system."

"And," added Alex, "there's far more W3 in play than we probably would've guessed six months ago."

"But not at the cost of having people engaged in the process," Julie added. "It feels like we're now ensuring people are engaged in the work that is most important."

Olivia nodded. "That is right. You're completing the workforce. How many times have you wished you had a couple more resources? This model frees up your current resources so you can complete the rest of the work."

She turned back to the rest of the group. "You made significant progress today. Next, we begin operationalizing this future. We will begin by assigning priorities, identifying capability gaps, and developing the roadmap. For now," she said, looking each member of the group in the eye, "pat yourself on the back. You all did great. This is what leadership of a significant change should look like."

Richard glanced again at the wall of future-state blueprints.

"It's the first time in a long time this team has created something new," David said. "Actually, let me rephrase that. This is the first time all of us, together, have built something new."

They all knew David was right, and anyone looking would have seen Carlos pat himself on the back.

Olivia said, "Go have a drink and enjoy a day well-spent. I will see you all tomorrow."

Chairs slid back, and the team stood, though most of them

lingered, talking through the accomplishments of the day. They all left the room energized, with Carlos inviting them to the local bar for a drink.

Richard knew the day was a success, overall; however, one key person was missing from every conversation. It frustrated him that Marcus couldn't be bothered to understand what was wrong with the company. Even if this wasn't the company he founded, he was not about to let it slide. It was unacceptable for the leader to behave this way.

Richard found Marcus in his office. His office door was cracked. Richard knocked once and stepped in without waiting. Marcus was hunched over his laptop, barely glancing up.

"Got a minute?" Richard asked, stepping in before Marcus could say no.

"What do you want?" Marcus asked, his tone flat.

Richard stayed standing. "I want to talk about why you weren't in the room today."

Marcus gave a short laugh. "Because I've got a business to run. We almost lost another customer today, and since I wasn't wasting my time with this nonsense, I was able to get them to stick around. My company is not a playground, and I am actually annoyed that my team decided to play with sticky notes and coloring books instead of getting their work done."

Richard paused and inhaled deeply before saying anything. He knew if he didn't take a minute, then what he had to say would come out wrong. "You think this is a luxury or that we are just playing games? Today was the work of the business. Today we took steps to determine whether you still have customers to keep in a year."

Marcus pushed his chair back from his desk. "Let me say this in a way you will understand… You don't run this company anymore, so don't walk in here and think you can tell me how to run it. If you really want to help, mind your own business and for heaven's sake, stop filling my team with crazy ideas."

Richard's jaw tightened. Usually, he was measured, even in conflict, but Marcus's dismissive tone had chipped away at his patience.

"My own business?" Richard said, his voice rising just enough to make Marcus look up. "Marcus, this is exactly my business. The only reason I'm here is that the company is sliding in the wrong direction, and the people counting on you don't see you leading them out of it."

"They're adults who know how to manage their own time. They don't need me showing them how to draw process maps."

"I think they need to see you to give a damn about the company!" Richard's voice rose. "They need to see you fighting for this company, not hiding behind excuses. You keep acting like these sessions are a distraction. Well, guess what? You are the only distraction, pretending the old way of running a company still works."

Marcus's face hardened, but he didn't answer.

Richard leaned over the desk, his tone dropping but still sharp. "Get off your ass, Marcus, and lead this company. That includes your people," He said, punctuating each sentence with a jab of his index finger onto the desk in front of Marcus.

The silence between them was heavy enough to cut through.

He stood up straight and crossed his arms. "Nate is going to ask me how it's going, and I'm going to tell him the truth, that you've checked out, that you've decided not to lead."

Marcus's face darkened. "You can tell Nate whatever the hell you want," he said, standing, pointing toward the door, "and you can get out of my office while you're at it."

Richard held Marcus's stare for a long beat, then turned and walked out.

Alex was waiting in the hallway. "That sounded intense."

Richard exhaled. "It was. He's not moving. Alex, enough is enough. We need to tell Nate that he has to go."

Alex nodded slowly. "I'll give Nate the update tonight."

Richard glanced back at Marcus's closed door. "So much for one last chance," he said quietly.

Back in his home office, Alex opened his laptop and hit the video call link. Nate's face filled the screen, with Dane sitting beside him.

"Hi, Alex. I am glad you called. It saved me from asking how things are going. Alright, give me the update," Nate said.

Alex began, "We've made real progress. The executive

team's finally starting to click, and even Emily seems on board with the direction. The team spent time understanding where the issues are and even mapped out a blueprint for the future. The executives left the room energized and headed to the bar for a drink."

"Well, it certainly sounds like it is going in the right direction," Nate said.

Alex's tone shifted. "There's one problem: Marcus. He continues to refuse to engage and lead his team through the difficult work. He didn't even show up for the workshop today. He holed up in his office running his old playbook, and we all know it's not working. After today, even his team knows they need a new operation manual. Richard confronted him about it, and that conversation didn't go well. The only person who still thinks the old model will work is Marcus, and we don't think he is changing his mind anytime soon."

Dane's expression hardened. "So, he just checked out?"

"Pretty much," Alex said. "If he's not willing to lead, we're wasting everyone's time."

Dane glanced at Nate, then back at Alex. "I've had it. I think the time has come to replace Marcus. We've given him every chance, and he's either blown it or ignored it."

Nate sighed, rubbing his forehead. "If we replace him, who do we get to step in?"

Dane didn't hesitate, "Alex, would you and Richard be open to coming back full-time?"

Alex blinked, caught off guard. "That's a big question."

"I know," Dane said, "but you've got the trust of the team now. They listen to you, and after what I've heard today, I'm not sure we've got time to find an outsider and hope they fit."

Alex didn't answer right away. "Let me talk to Richard. I think he will want to see the output of the workshop and if we can turn the company around before it's too late."

Nate nodded. "Fair enough, but think about it. If Marcus won't do the job, someone has to, and we don't have the time or luxury to run a six-month search."

Alex closed the call, staring out the window for a moment. If Marcus was out, the next move could change everything for the company– for good or bad.

That night, Richard and Kathy settled into their usual seats at the kitchen table. Richard looked tired but content.

"How was your day?" She asked.

"It was eventful," he said with a sigh. "We continued with the workshop, and the executive team seemed to get on board, which was reassuring. How about you? How was your day?"

Kathy looked at Richard and said, "It was actually interesting. At our staff meeting this morning, Mark introduced a new dashboard, which tracks real-time community needs. It pulls in open data from global humanitarian organizations, and lets us proactively spot where the biggest need is so that we can reroute funds and resources faster."

"That sounds pretty amazing," Richard said with honest interest.

"It is," she admitted, "but I had to ask him about the numbers. We can take action based on them, but I needed more context. I really wanted to see the story behind the numbers so we aren't spinning our wheels."

Richard smiled. "That sounds like you."

"Mark said, 'Well, we are giving you the numbers so you can overlay your judgment. I can get you the numbers, but they only provide information. You have to make the decisions based on the information at your fingertips.' Then Samantha chimed in: 'Oh, I see. It's the numbers for the people. We still have to use our experience to analyze and interpret them appropriately.'

"I actually wrote that down—'It's the numbers for the people.' Later, I put it into my AI assistant's prompt, 'Use this phrase in a donor newsletter intro,' and it gave me something really good. I was pleasantly surprised at the output. I think I even smiled when reading what it gave me."

Richard raised an eyebrow. "You're an AI convert now?"

She laughed, "It feels like I finally understand, even a little, the power of this tool. I am certainly less afraid of it."

"That's huge, dear. Not surprising, it's the same thing I'm trying to get across to the executive team. AI is expanding what we can do if we implement it correctly."

Kathy nodded. "Speaking of expanding, they gave me a project today that I'm pretty excited about. They asked me to research new CRMs for the team. As you know, the one we have is a dinosaur."

Richard looked at her. "Oh yes, I've heard about your love-hate relationship with it. You know, you should let AI help you with the research. Maybe have it compile the top options, the best companies, and then build a pros and cons list for each. I bet it will save you hours of legwork."

She smirked. "Look at you, coaching me on AI adoption."

"Someone's got to," he teased. "Besides, you're halfway there already. Might as well finish the journey."

Right then, Richard's cell phone rang. He looked at Kathy and said, "It's Alex," and took the call.

"Hey, Alex. How'd the call with Nate go?"

Kathy could hear Alex on the phone. "It was very productive, though it took an unexpected turn. Dane was also on the call, so I walked them both through everything we've done so far, including the workshops and the blueprint work. I let them know that the team's finally starting to gel," He paused. "Well, not the whole team," he said with a rueful laugh.

"Marcus," Richard said flatly. Marcus's actions still aggravated him.

"Marcus," Alex confirmed. "I told them he refused to join the sessions today, and he keeps trying the same old methods, which certainly are not working."

Richard stood up and paced to the back door, staring out into the dark yard. "And?"

"Dane didn't take it well. He said, and I quote, 'It's time to replace Marcus. We've given him every chance, and he's either blown it or ignored it.'"

Richard let out a slow breath. "I can't say I disagree with the conclusion."

"Then Nate asked the obvious question: who steps in if Marcus is out?" Alex paused again, this time longer. "Dane looked right at me through the screen and said, 'Would you and Richard be open to coming back full-time?'"

Richard froze, hand on the doorknob. He had not expected that. "What did you say?"

"I said yes."

"No, seriously, what did you tell them?" Richard was not

going to fall for Alex's joke.

You could almost hear Alex's smile through the phone. "I told them we'd talk about it, but we needed to see the outcome of the workshop. I, for one, am not convinced the company is fixable, but, you should know, they're serious."

Chapter Ten
Beyond Headcount

A couple of days later, Richard followed the scent of fresh coffee into the kitchen, his hair damp from his shower. Kathy sat at the table, scrolling through the morning news on her tablet.

"You're up early," she said, glancing over her glasses. "I figured after getting in so late last night, you'd sleep in."

He poured his coffee and plopped down into the chair across from her. "Yeah, it was a late night. Alex, Olivia, and I stayed longer than planned. We covered a lot. More than I expected."

Kathy closed her tablet. "Okay. Give me the details. How is everything going?"

Richard smiled. "Olivia had us map out the new org structure yesterday, and even wants us to give job descriptions for every role on it. Not just for the employees, but for every bot and AI agent, too. Oh, and get this— she wants us to name the AI agents as well."

Kathy looked at him. "You're telling me you're about to give a robot a name and job title?"

"Technically, they're not robots; they are software systems, but yes," he said, smirking. "That is what Olivia wants us to do. She says it makes them part of the team and forces us to define what they actually are, rather than treating them like mysterious black boxes. Weirdly, it makes sense. If we can't describe what they do, how can we manage what their output is supposed to look like?"

Kathy stirred her coffee. "I guess that makes sense. If you name the new puppy, you're more likely to take care of it."

"That is one way to look at it," Richard said, chuckling. "Except these puppies process invoices, manage scheduling, and run analytics."

"As long as you aren't trying to replace the human relationship with a tool. With all the work-from-home, it might be easier for employees to prefer talking to a bot to a human. I keep reading stories of how relationships get impacted because one spouse or another is getting too emotionally attached to AI."

"I hadn't considered that angle since most of the bots and AI agents they have implemented don't have the interactive capabilities like Alexa or ChatGPT, but you bring up an interesting point. I will make sure to discuss that with Olivia."

Her smile faded slightly. "You sound," she paused, "invested in this process."

He leaned back. "That's the other thing. You already know that Dane and Nate asked Alex and me to consider stepping back in full-time. We discussed what that would look like at length, as well."

Kathy set her mug down, the clink sharper than usual. "I bet that took Olivia by surprise."

"As much of a surprise as the rest of us. I asked her opinion on the topic. She didn't give me an answer, just asked me a bunch of questions to think about. Do I really want to jump back into the day-to-day grind? Do I want to run a company I don't own, answering to a PE firm?"

"Where's your head at?" Kathy prompted, lips pursed.

"I don't know. There's part of me that misses the seat, but it's a different kind of leadership when you're not the owner. There are a lot more guardrails and a lot less freedom to make decisions the way you believe best. Besides, we'd be inheriting a turnaround, so it will not be an easy path forward."

"Richard," she started gently, "you've always excelled when you could make decisions, set the vision, and get the right people on board. Now you'd be answering to the PE guys and be at the mercy of their expectations. You won't have the final say in everything."

"Honestly, I keep wondering if I am ready for that kind of role."

Kathy nodded. "My main concern is that you'll be working for someone else, and I'm not sure if you want to do that. If you are prepared for that, then I will be fully behind you. I just want to make sure you are sure of what you're getting into."

He looked down at his coffee. "Yes, I need to make sure I'm okay following someone else's direction. I also need to remember that PE play by different rules. They march to monthly EBITDA targets and pull the value out as quickly as they can."

"Are you willing to reshape the role enough that it feels like you are still in the driver's seat? Just remember, every car comes with an owner's manual you didn't write."

Richard smiled faintly at that, though his eyes stayed distant. "I'll have to think about that."

She reached across the table and squeezed his hand. "I know you will. Just make sure the next seat you take is one you actually want to sit in, not just one you know how to fill."

Kathy let go of his hand and sat back, a small smile returning to her face. Changing the topic, she said, "You're naming AI agents now? Next, will you have them make your coffee?"

Richard grinned. "Olivia didn't say how far to take it, but knowing her, she'll probably have us set quarterly goals for the bots. Heck, she may even want us to have virtual team-building exercises with them."

Kathy chuckled. "I guess you need to start coming up with some names for these new imaginary employees."

"Got any suggestions?" Richard asked.

She pretended to think about the question seriously. "Let's see. If I had an AI agent at CI, I just might call it Grantilda. You know, like Matilda, but one that helps me write grants."

Richard laughed, nearly spitting his coffee out. "Grantilda? That's terrible, and strangely perfect."

"Oh, there is so much potential with AI names," Kathy said. "We could call the events AI PartyBot Pete. And the donor database? Phil the Philanthropy Assistant. He'd wear virtual bow ties, of course."

Richard shook his head. "I guess I need to up my game before the next executive meeting. Otherwise, I might show up with a list of names sounding like storybook characters."

"That's the point," she said. "If you're going to lead humans and machines, you might as well give the machines a little personality, have fun with it."

He raised his mug in a toast. "To Grantilda."

She clinked her mug against his. "To Grantilda."

Kathy settled into her home office, tucking her legs under her chair and nudging aside a stack of donor reports to make room for her laptop. The house was quiet; Richard had left for the day, the kids were at school, and even the dogs were napping.

She opened her AI assistant, the interface coming to life on the screen. For the last week, she'd been using it namelessly, but something about Richard's story this morning– Olivia telling the executive team to name their AI agents– stuck with her.

Kathy typed, "Good morning," into the prompt.

The AI GPT responded, "Good morning, Kathy. How can I help you today?"

She hesitated, then typed, "Before we get started, would it be okay if I gave you a name?"

She wasn't sure why she was asking, but it felt impersonal not to ask. The AI responded after a brief pause, as if the system were considering the request. "Of course you can. I've been called many things by many people, but never by a name that's uniquely mine. What name are you thinking of? If you do not have a name in mind, I can help you brainstorm some options. Would you like me to help you brainstorm name suggestions?"

Kathy typed, "What do you think about the name Grantilda?"

"Grantilda. I like it. It sounds both distinguished and approachable. You can call me that from now on."

Kathy typed, "Great. I'm researching new CRM systems for my nonprofit. I would like you to help me pull together the best systems, what their costs are, and help me make a case to implement the new tool."

Grantilda responded instantly, "I would start by considering the cost and system capability. Many of these systems have integrated AI agents that can automate donor communications and track giving patterns. It also allows you to expand your donor outreach without additional resources. It means you would expect to see an ROI by avoiding adding more people."

Kathy sat back, thinking about Grantilda's response. She realized they could handle a bigger donor base without burning out the team. She then typed, "How does it do that?"

Grantilda replied, "The system can send personalized thank-you notes, schedule follow-up calls at the perfect time, and even flag when a donor might be ready for a larger gift, automatically. Do you want me to suggest some CRM software that incorporates AI bots?"

Kathy's mind was already racing ahead. The right system could give them the reach of a much larger organization, without the headcount. She and her teammates could focus on building relationships instead of chasing data.

She then pulled up three CRM demos she'd bookmarked and typed. "Can you review these systems and tell me the pros, cons, and AI-driven features that would allow us to deliver more results without substantial cost to the organization?"

Grantilda's tone didn't change, but Kathy swore it somehow sounded more interested. A chart appeared, with each system outlined and its benefits and drawbacks.

Grantilda followed up, "Do you want me to help you build the justification for the investment?"

"Yes," Kathy typed. "I need something solid for the CEO and the board. How can I explain spending more without sounding like I've lost my mind?"

Grantilda proceeded to provide the data Kathy was requesting. Time seemed to pass as Kathy engaged with the research and examined the opportunities from every angle. Kathy looked up and realized she had spent almost an hour, but had a whole framework put together. She expected it to take weeks to get to this point. Then she had a thought.

She typed, "It sounds like I'm hiring a new staff member without the extra costs."

"That is one way to look at it," Grantilda said.

Kathy laughed. "I like it," she said out loud.

The realization began to settle over her, not just in her head, but in her gut. She was seeing the value of this Third Workforce that Richard had been talking about. This software would enable the non-profit to help more children and others in need without requiring additional resources.

She pictured pitching it to her CEO and telling him she wants a new teammate, but this one will be a system that can easily take on more work than a single employee can.

Kathy glanced at the list of CRM contenders on her screen and understood the benefit of the Third Workforce.

Richard pushed open the door, and the smell of dark roast coffee and fresh pastries filled his senses instantly. Alex was already there, nursing a coffee, and scrolling through something on his tablet.

"You're early," Richard said, sliding into the seat across from him.

Alex smirked. "Old habits. I like getting here before the morning rush hits."

Richard decided he wanted something and said, "Do you want anything. The smell of coffee is making me want a cup."

Alex shook his head as Richard went to order his black drip coffee and a coffee cake.

When Richard returned, he said, "Olivia's on her way home. That leaves us to figure out, well, everything. Let's discuss what Dane and Nate want from us. Where's your head at?"

Alex set down his cup. "I'm tired of feeling like a janitor cleaning up other people's financial messes. When I started fractional work, it was fun; I could parachute in, grab the low-hanging fruit, stop the bleeding, and move on to the next gig. I could go home without worrying about the next board meeting.

"I miss what we had. We were building toward something bigger than ourselves. A legacy we could leave behind and be proud of. Honestly, I miss that. I miss working with you every day."

Richard nodded slowly. "Does that mean you would like to give it a go?"

Alex smiled. "Yeah, I think so. But the bigger question is, what about you? And maybe even more importantly, what about Kathy?"

Richard stared into his coffee. "Part of me wants to jump

in. I like the idea of working the day-to-day again, leading, fixing, and building. I like feeling needed. This time," he said, shaking his head, "we won't be the owners. We'll be answering to Dane and Nate. That's a different kind of leadership. They'll want results on their timeline, in their way. That could box us in."

Alex studied him for a moment. "We've both been in this situation in the past. I know, it's been a while, but we can figure out how to work our magic in the confines of their way of doing business."

Richard chuckled softly. "You always did have a knack for bending the rules without snapping them."

"Sometimes you have to." He took a sip of coffee. "It's not like we haven't been here before. I still remember sitting in that coffee shop in Silicon Valley, sketching out our plans on napkins with no idea how we would implement them. We had a big vision and a firm belief we could make this idea work."

Richard smiled faintly at the thought. "We were much younger then and either fearless or stupid."

"I say both," Alex said with a grin. "But it worked out just fine, didn't it? It's because we knew we had each other's backs and that brings a level of confidence into any situation."

Thinking back to those early days, Richard said, "If we do this, we have to be clear about why we would come back to our old company. I don't want to jump back into the game for nostalgia's sake. I want to be sure we can actually turn this company around, in a way that leaves it better than we found it."

"I agree. If nothing else, we can shore up the leadership team and processes so the company continues the fight. Worst-case scenario, we can't turn it completely around, and we step away again."

Richard looked out the window at the street, then back at Alex. He began to shake his head slowly and said, "If you're in, I'm in."

"I'm in. I want something that I can really sink my teeth into again. Something that I can build up, not just play repairman. Most of all, I want to do it with you, as we used to."

Richard's shoulders loosened, like he'd been holding the tension for days. "Then we have one more big decision: Emily. Do we keep her as CFO?"

Alex nodded his head. "She's very capable and experienced. I like her for the organization. I think the jury is still out on whether she can break out of her silo thinking. If she can, I'm fine with her staying in the role. You will have your hands full with the PE guys, so let me take on a chief administration role, covering Finance, HR, and IT. They are going to need to work together for this to work."

Richard took that in, then said, "It sure feels like we're building the company all over again."

Alex raised his cup in a small toast. "Then let's make sure we do it right...again."

The conference room was all glass and angles; modern, minimal, and just cold enough to make the occupants aware that deals made here were about numbers first, people second. Richard and Alex sat on one side of the long table. Across from them, Dane adjusted his cufflinks while Nate scrolled through something on his tablet.

Dane looked up first. "Gentlemen, glad you could make it."

Richard returned his look, saying, "We appreciate your time."

"Of course," Nate said without looking up. "Let me get right to the point. You know this business better than anyone. I know this is highly unusual, but we need measurable results fast. We would waste too much time going to the market to find a replacement, and then there would be more time lost on the learning curve. You two are the logical choice."

Alex leaned forward slightly. "We understand that, which is why we don't want to come in as hired guns. If this is going to work, we need to step back in full-time; however, it will require the right structure and incentive plan to make it worth our while."

Dane raised an eyebrow. "Go on. What are you thinking?"

Richard jumped in, "I'll take on the CEO role, and Alex will step in as the CAO. We'll run day-to-day, drive the turnaround, and deliver the results you need. If we're doing that, we want meaningful equity. We want a real stake in the upside we're going to create."

Nate set his tablet down. "Equity's expensive. We could just pay you well and keep you motivated that way."

Alex shook his head. "That's not good enough. If you want

us to be committed to this company's success, equity makes that possible. Both of us can walk away from a salary, since there is no true commitment to a salary."

Dane crossed his arms. "Okay, I can understand that. What are you asking for?"

Richard didn't hesitate when he said, "Ten percent, split between us."

The silence stretched long enough for the HVAC hum to become noticeable.

Nate leaned back. "That's rich. We've got capital at risk, and you're coming in after the fact. We could see maybe three percent. Total."

Alex let out a small laugh, not out of humor but disbelief.

"Three percent is what you give a VP who sticks around for a liquidity event. We're talking about rebuilding the company, restoring value to your investment, and then growing it. You're asking us to make decisions like owners, so we need to be owners."

Dane leaned forward, voice low, "And if we say no?"

"Then we keep doing what we're doing," Richard replied. "You find someone else willing to burn themselves out for a base salary and a pat on the back."

The tension in the room shifted. Dane and Nate exchanged a look, one of those silent exchanges that lasts two seconds but communicates a paragraph.

Nate spoke first, "Five percent. With performance triggers. You hit the first-year targets, you get another two. We'll tie the rest to EBITDA milestones."

Richard considered it, then looked at Alex. "What do you think?"

"Seven percent total with the appropriate performance gates? Yeah, I'm good with that number."

Richard turned back to them. "Alright, but let's get it in writing and establish clear timelines and targets, including a clause that you won't move the goalposts for the first three years. We also want a change-of-control clause in there with a three-year payout. Oh, and we want to pick our own team."

Dane nodded. "Absolutely, we don't want to get into the details of your talent. As for the change-of-control clause, our standard is two years for your level. If you are okay with that, then we've got ourselves a deal."

Richard and Alex nodded their agreement with the clause, and Nate said, "We will get the lawyers to write up the contracts."

They stood and shook hands across the table. Everyone felt like they got what they wanted. Nate and Dane landed two experienced operators to turn the business around. Richard and Alex gained a sizable ownership in the business.

As Richard and Alex walked out into the brisk air, Alex exhaled, "Well, we're back in it."

The black sedan navigated through the late afternoon traffic on the way to the airport. Richard sat behind the driver, his mind reflecting on the conversation in the conference room. Alex sat next to him, jacket off, tie loosened, staring out the window, watching the cityscape pass by.

Alex broke the silence and said, "I still can't believe we got them to seven percent."

"Well, they gave us five with an upside if we get through the performance gates."

"You think we can hit those numbers?"

Richard glanced at him. "I sure hope so. I know we have faced bigger challenges before, but you just never know how things will turn out."

Alex let out a breath, leaning his head back against the seat. "I am at peace with our decision. It almost feels like we're coming home. Even if it's not the same home we left."

"I feel it too. I am keenly aware that we are not the same leaders either. Yes, we're older, but hopefully a little bit wiser. "

They rode in silence again for a bit before Richard spoke, "Alright then. Tomorrow, we begin mapping out our first ninety days. When we walk through the doors in a couple of days, we will be going one-hundred miles per hour."

Alex chuckled, "I wouldn't have it any other way."

The car took the departure lane toward the airport as both men were resolved to face the next part of the journey together.

Chapter Eleven
Designing the System

The reaction was instant; a few gasps and surprised looks on the executive team's faces. David was the first to speak, "Can I ask what happened? We just saw Marcus this morning."

Dane kept his voice calm, "This wasn't a snap decision. We've been evaluating performance and direction for some time. Over the last few weeks, the conclusion was clear, and a change at the top was necessary."

Carlos leaned forward. "Was this about strategy or execution?"

"A bit of both," Nate said, stepping in. "I know this kind of transition raises a lot of questions and several concerns. It's unsettling when leadership changes abruptly. I want to assure you and to have you hear this from me, the decision had the future of the company in mind, and we believe Richard is going to move quickly to get us back on track."

"What about Marcus? Did he see this coming?" Emily said, frowning.

Dane hesitated for a moment. "He knew there were performance concerns. These moments are never easy, and I don't take them lightly, but leadership is about what's best for the organization, even when it's uncomfortable."

The room quieted.

David cleared his throat. "Does this change the strategy we've been building on for the past two years?"

"The direction won't change overnight, but there will be adjustments," Alex said. "We've got to align with the realities of our competitors and where the market is heading."

Carlos tilted his head. "And our roles? Are we expected to change direction, too?"

Richard stepped in, "I know this is a lot to take in. Change rarely feels convenient, and the truth is, this is a season of change for the company. Sometimes a new season asks more of us than we expect."

He paused, glancing around the table to be sure he had everyone's attention. "When I was traveling in California a few years back, I visited the Nelder Grove Sequoias after the 2017 fires. You'd think that a low-intensity fire— one that leaves the trees standing—would be better for them; however, it turns out that those trees don't regenerate under those conditions. The seeds stay locked in their cones, waiting."

He leaned forward. "It's the high-intensity fires— the ones that take the old giants down— that open the cones, release the seeds, and produce a hundred times more new growth. The very thing that feels like destruction is what creates the possibility for a forest that's even stronger and more alive."

The room was silent. Even Dane, arms crossed, seemed to stand in anticipation of what Richard would say next.

"So, yes," Richard continued, "this is uncomfortable. For some of you, this may even be unsettling, but I want you to see it for what it is: an opening. A chance to rethink, regrow, and build something bigger than any of us could have managed in the shade of what was."

Julie softly asked, "What does that mean for us today?"

"It means we keep moving forward and take the next step of the Talent Trek. Olivia will guide us through it. In the coming weeks, we'll begin making decisions that will shape the next decade of this company. But know this, you're here because we believe you can not only survive the high heat, but also come out better for it."

Richard paused and said, "Here's what you can expect from me. I will get in the mud with you, not sit behind a desk and bark orders. Don't worry, I don't intend to micro-manage anyone. If you lead, then you can run your department. I will be transparent and keep you informed about everything I can. I expect you to do the same to the rest of the team and me. We are going to succeed or fail together. We can't afford any lone wolves making a mess of things."

Alex chimed in, "I will be here, as well. We will discuss my role at a later time. The good news is Olivia will keep leading the Talent Trek transformation."

Richard informed the team that Dane and Nate would have to leave. They would then take a break until the scheduled time for the next session. The meeting broke, chairs scraping across the floor as people gathered their belongings. Some slipped out quickly, wanting to process the news in private. Others lingered.

Julie was the first to approach. "Richard, I am not sure how best to ask this, but are we keeping the strategic initiatives Marcus launched?"

Richard smiled faintly. "We'll review each initiative together before making changes. If something's working, we'll keep it. If not, we'll need to adjust. I don't plan on blindsiding anyone. I believe in a collaborative, team approach."

She sighed, visibly relieved.

Carlos hung back by the coffee pot. When Richard made his way over, Carlos said quietly, "I'll be honest, I personally liked Marcus, but we've been drifting for the last few months. If you can give us a real north star again, I'm all in."

Richard met his gaze. "That's exactly the plan. I'll need you to challenge me if you think we're veering off course. Can you do that?"

"Deal."

Carlos shook his hand and left the room. Richard glanced around the room and saw Emily standing near the door, arms folded. He walked over to her and was not surprised when she took the direct approach, asking, "Is Alex taking my job as CFO?"

Richard responded, "No, you will remain CFO. I will, however, have Alex step into the Chief Administration Officer role to help me connect all of the dots while straightening this ship."

Her eyes went wide. "I see."

"Alex and I are going to make sure Finance has a seat at the table for every major decision. You'll have visibility into and input on any initiative before we move forward. We need you on this team."

"Thanks, I appreciate it," Emily said as she walked out the door, still surprised that she would remain on the team.

Brianne now got up from her seat, where she had been patiently waiting, and walked over to Richard. "Should I be packing my bags, too? I know you aren't a fan of all the automation and AI I've been driving."

Richard wasn't sure what to expect from Brianne. Her directness, however, was not on his bingo card. "Look, Brianne, I am a fan of AI, automation, and finding better ways to do our work. I also am a fan of implementing it the right way. Going forward, we will focus on change management, and that is non-negotiable, but it won't stop the progress in what you have been doing."

"Alright," she said, taking a deep, steadying breath. "I see now the importance of bringing employees on board with what we are implementing and providing some training around the tools, instead of assuming they'll be able to manage it and figure it out themselves. I'll get with my team to strategize which training sessions need to be held and to plan some open-forum discussions around the implementation of these tools. Thank you for the chance to prove myself."

Richard chuckled, "That sounds like a good start, and as long as you remain willing to change and grow, and help your team meet your KPIs, you are welcome on the team."

"Thank you," Brianne said and headed to the door.

By the time the conference room emptied, Richard sensed the leadership team was in a good place. He wasn't naive enough to think it would be easy from here on out, but he was encouraged that the transition went as well as expected.

A cloud still hung over the conference room after Marcus's departure announcement. Olivia was figuring out how to balance keeping momentum and giving the team room to process the news.

"Thank you for leaning into this process so far," she began.

"Last time, we tackled job descriptions. You've now defined the work, established job descriptions, and named your AI teammates. Today, we take the next step in evaluating your talent. We won't be putting names in boxes yet. We will begin by talking through the skills and strengths that enable the organization to succeed. We will also have to capture any gaps in our future state."

Emily asked, "You mean, assessing whether the people we have actually have the skills to pull this off?"

"Yes," Olivia said, nodding. "A workforce without the right skills will stumble, no matter how good the vision or strategy is."

As the executives talked through their teams, a picture began to emerge of the organization's strengths. Not unexpectedly, HR was abundant with employees who focused on relationships and problem-solving, though they were concerned about what AI meant for their jobs. The Operations team had embraced automation and AI, but lacked the depth of understanding needed to challenge the numbers. Marketing continued to be amazing with their creativity and storytelling, and Finance brought the numbers to life as well as any finance team Emily had led. However, she knew collaboration was a significant gap for them.

The executives realized that, unfortunately, the breakneck push toward AI had come at a high cost to the employee base. Looking at it now, they appreciated that attrition created a gap in experienced talent who understood the legacy systems. The systems that were still critical in running the business.

No one questioned the teams' capabilities. For the most part, each department was accomplishing what it needed to, but the work had changed, and the expectations had, as well. The gap in the future state capability became much clearer as they discussed.

Richard had been listening quietly and finally spoke up, "Here's my takeaway. We've all underestimated how much capability-building this season requires. As we have learned over the last few weeks, we can't simply graft AI into our old ways of working. We must ask ourselves, 'What kind of talent do we need to maximize our new way of working?' It is clear we have to rebuild our talent base."

The room went quiet. Even Carlos stopped fiddling with his pen.

Olivia picked up the thread, "That's exactly where we are.

It's uncomfortable and potentially disruptive. Suppose we can be honest about our gaps, put the right people in the right places, and equip them with the right skills; the next generation of this workforce can multiply in strength like never before. You just mentioned some of your organizational gaps. We now need to think about which of those gaps are most important to prioritize first."

"I'm not sure what you are asking of us. Do you want us to build new training programs?" Julie asked.

Olivia smiled. "Not just training programs, though I imagine in some cases training will be necessary. It's as much about leadership as anything else. Everyone will have to manage differently in a W3 world. Some of the gaps I heard were digital fluency, data interpretation, cross-functional collaboration, AI literacy, and systems thinking.

"You can't fix everything at once, so we need to prioritize which capabilities are most important to fix? Which gaps will have the greatest positive impact in unlocking the organization's value? "

Emily tilted her head. "Are we ranking skills?"

Olivia replied, "We aren't so much ranking the skills as we are trying to figure out how to prioritize the skills. Let's assume all of the skills are important, but which drives value the fastest? Look, every organization has gaps, and the best teams don't chase all of them at once; they focus on the ones that move the business forward the fastest."

The team debated each of the key gaps and eventually agreed to focus on AI literacy, digital fluency, and data interpretation.

Richard then said, "Who are your top players? Who's ready to lead these capability shifts?"

A long pause. The silence was uncomfortable. Emily stared at her notes. Carlos cleared his throat but said nothing. Julie shifted in her chair.

Finally, David spoke up, "Richard, we let the talent review process drop a couple of years ago as a company. I have kept the process up in my organization; however, I am not sure we know who our best are."

The others turned to him.

David squirmed a little and said, "What? I've maintained the discipline of running a 9-box with my team every year, so I know who has high potential, who can stretch, and where my risks lie. I can name the people right now who could lead AI literacy in Ops."

Olivia's face lit up. "That's exactly the point. You can't steer transformation if you don't know your bench strength. David's ahead here, but the rest of you need to catch up."

Julie hung her head. "HR should be leading this practice, but we've neglected it. I should have been more direct and pushed it." She took the opportunity to take accountability for not focusing on talent, which the team appreciated.

"Then this is your wake-up call," Richard said. "If we don't know who our top talent is, we're not going to get very far. This is a critical step in our journey to transform this organization."

Olivia gestured toward the board. "Here's your next assignment. Identify your top talent. Do the work David has been doing. Bring back a clear picture of who can lead in this new model. At the end of the day, job descriptions mean nothing without capable people to fill them."

The team sat back, the weight of the task sinking in.

Olivia thought for a minute and added, "I am going to call an audible for the rest of the day. We need to identify the top talent within the organization. Let's take a break. Grab your computers or any notes you have on your teams. Then, I will facilitate us through a talent review so we can have a better picture of your top people."

When the team returned, Olivia led them through the 9-box talent review process,[1] discussing how to consider potential, performance, and the roles most critical to success in the months ahead. First, they talked about their critical roles. Olivia stressed the importance of getting these roles right. When staffed with top talent, these roles supercharge the organization's growth and speed. She explained that if you don't get the right people in them, everything else slows down. There was a good bit of dialogue, debate, and discussion until finally, they settled on the top roles in the new organization that would need the best and brightest talent.

The team identified the critical roles. Olivia moved on to the actual talent review, where she went through each box as the team began assigning its members to them. The discussion wasn't always comfortable, with heated debates and a few tense moments during which soul-searching occurred. In those disagreements, the leaders came around to acknowledge the underperforming

1 See Appendix for reference

employees. For the first time in years, the executive team spoke candidly about talent.

By the time the sun began dipping lower in the conference room windows, the team had identified their top talent and realized they had lost many great people over the years. There were some significant gaps, especially when they overlaid top talent to the critical roles they had identified earlier.

"We can't afford to leave these seats empty or underpowered any longer," Richard said, looking at the board.

"It seems pretty clear to me," Emily added, "that if we can't get the right talent into these roles, we will all be looking for new jobs."

Olivia had an uncharacteristic frown on her face. Only Richard and Alex noticed it.

"What are you thinking, Olivia?" Alex asked.

After a pause, Olivia said, "I am actually surprised at how few top talent we have. We clearly don't have enough to fill every critical role or deliver what we need to. We may need to take a slightly different short-term approach. My recommendation is to select the best talent and create three Talent Teams to enable them to develop a strategy and take necessary action. In the meantime, I think Julie's recruiting team will need to go find some top talent to fill in the gaps."

Slowly, nods followed around the table.

"I agree. I'm not sure if you continued using Talent Teams in our absence, so we will go over them briefly," Richard addressed the room. "Talent teams are designed to provide top talent an opportunity to accelerate their capabilities. If they succeed, the company succeeds. If they fail, well, let's just say the stakes are high."

Olivia said, "Here's how we'll organize the teams. Each of you will name two people. They won't simply be your representatives; we need them to think about the enterprise, not just their department. They'll be responsible for turning what we've built here into reality."

One by one, the names went up on the board. Each organization handed over top talent to the enterprise, knowing it might be painful for the team, but that it was necessary to engage a broader population of the organization.

Olivia stepped back. "This is your vanguard. They're the ones building the bridge to where you're going."

Richard scanned the board, then turned back to the team. "I want to make sure everyone is clear that it's our job to make sure they succeed." Nodding heads and murmurs of agreement rose around the room.

"Now that you've identified your top talent," Olivia said, "we need to identify and assign them to the right strategic projects. What are the top priorities where we could accelerate our transformation by leveraging this pool of talent?"

Carlos leaned forward. "We've got dozens of gaps, how do we choose?"

"That's the point," Richard said. "We can't attack everything at once. We need leverage, and we have to identify the top two or three initiatives to get us started. As Olivia mentioned, if we get them right, we move the whole company forward."

Julie raised her hand slightly. "What about structure? Half the tension in this room has centered on the lack of talent, the new roles that are needed, and the ideal reporting structure. We would really benefit from establishing a new org structure and understanding how W1, W2, and W3 would integrate."

"I'll second that," David heartily agreed. "My team is asking every day, 'Who owns what now?' If we can't answer clearly, they'll stop listening."

Olivia turned back to the whiteboard and wrote 'Organization Structure' and said, "Good. That's one."

Carlos spoke, "AI management has come up in every single session. None of us have leaders who know how to manage the Third Workforce. We can't roll this out responsibly unless we train managers to do it well."

Emily sighed, "I hate to admit it, but he's right. My finance managers are clueless about how to manage digital colleagues. If we don't train them, we will be in a world of hurt six months from now."

"AI Management Training," Olivia wrote in block letters. "That's two."

Brianne spoke after a moment of thought, "What about governance? Employees are experimenting with new tools every day. We need to create standards and establish oversight. I am not talking only about IT governance. I am thinking about the organization's governance of the tools."

Richard added, "I like it and agree. Governance permeates every aspect of the organization, including how employees interact with the tools. Besides, if the auditors ever asked us how we monitor AI in our processes, we'd have nothing to show them."

"Or worse," Alex said. "We'd have to admit we don't monitor it at all."

Olivia wrote down and underlined the third item: governance. "Yes, establishing guardrails for AI on process oversight and even relationships is critical. I think this is a good list to start with. Organization structure, AI management training, and governance. These will be your Talent Teams."

Julie glanced at the list of names on the board. "Who do we select for which team?"

David spoke first, "The last time we did this, we nominated people from our departments for the different teams. Are we doing it the same way?

"If so, I think Jenna has a good eye for organizational structure. I would say put her on the org structure team. I would also nominate Luis for that team as well, since he knows how work actually flows on the floor."

"Raj and Tanya should go on the AI management training team," Julie said. "Raj has already been poking around with automation in recruiting, and Tanya's a natural trainer; people will listen to her."

"Alina will be perfect for the Governance team. She came from a compliance-heavy industry before joining us, and she naturally thinks about risk. Pair her with Mark from Finance, and you've got two people who will make sure we have the right controls in place," Carlos said, tapping the table.

Emily added, "I'll back that. Mark is tough-minded, sometimes to a fault, but governance needs a watchdog."

Olivia said, "Excellent. Now we need to build out the details and sell them on the opportunity."

The late-summer air was warm, carrying the hum of newly hatched cicadas. Richard and Kathy sat on the back patio, watching the light fade behind the trees.

"You look less stressed tonight," Richard said.

Kathy smiled. "It was a good day. Grantilda and I finally finished the case for the new CRM project. Honestly, I couldn't have pulled it together without her."

Richard grinned at the way she said it, as if Grantilda were just another member of her team. "You're officially on a first-name basis with your AI co-worker now?"

"Don't start," Kathy said, laughing, "but yes. I'm still getting used to it. At first, it felt like a threat, or at best, a gimmick. Then, today, Grantilda helped me organize our entire donor engagement history, spot patterns, and even prepare the slides. I presented it to the CEO this afternoon, and she loved where I was going. She said it was the clearest strategic proposal she's seen in months."

"That's incredible," Richard said. "It sounds like you're starting to see what's possible."

Kathy nodded, looking out at the fireflies starting to blink across the yard. "I guess I am. AI is helping me become better at what I do, and honestly, it's kind of exciting."

Richard thought about the irony of their individual situations. They were both, in their own worlds, yet learning the same lesson about using AI thoughtfully, helpfully, to put people first. When you stop resisting the change, you can lead it, not fear it.

Chapter Twelve
The People Who Hold It Together

The morning sun lit the café. At one table in the back, three notepads lay open as the newly appointed Talent Team leaders sat, waiting for the meeting to begin.

Richard cleared his throat and said, "I am sure you heard from your leaders that the last couple of weeks have been intense. Workshops, sticky notes, debates, and more diagrams than anyone should have to look at, but I want this to be a conversation to discuss how the three of you were selected to lead the efforts in creating a new future for the company."

Jenna nodded, keeping her professional persona intact. "We understand. I think I speak for all of us that we are honored to be selected and will do everything we can to get this right."

Alex said, "Good, because your roles as Talent Team leaders need to be more than leading a task or a project. You're translating the company's future blueprint from paper into reality. If this works, it's because you made it work."

Richard continued, "When we picked you, it wasn't because you had the most senior titles. It's because we believe you are the best we have at the company."

Tanya raised her hand slightly and then quickly put it down

with a sheepish smile. "What exactly are we driving?"

Richard smiled. "That is the million-dollar question, isn't it? Jenna, your focus will be on the organizational structure. With all the changes, you have to make sure the new design works as we expect. Tanya, you'll head up AI management training. We recognize that our employees need to learn the good, the bad, and the ugly of AI, including how to manage it effectively. In some cases, even manage it like a teammate.

"And Mark, you'll run the governance team. We must put the right guardrails in place so we don't lose control in the process. There is still a lot we don't know about AI, and I want to make sure we have the right eyes on the critical junctions in processes and decisions. I don't want a system running amok."

"You can't treat these as side projects," Alex said. "They are too important to the company, and that means you are not alone in these efforts. Each of you will build a cross-functional team of top talent. If you require any additional skills or capabilities, please let us know. Your job is to lead them, guide them, and deliver the expected outcomes."

The implications of their new roles set in. Jenna spoke up, "Are these teams on top of our normal responsibilities, or am I understanding correctly that these teams are to replace our current roles temporarily?"

"They will temporarily replace them as you work to serve the greater good and growth of the company," Alex said.

"We're basically spearheading the transformation of the whole company," Jenna said, processing the weight of these roles.

"That's right," Richard replied. "You're the ones who will show the rest of the organization this isn't another corporate experiment. We will transform the company, because if we don't, we won't have a company for much longer. All that to say, I want us to leave here with an understanding of why this matters and how you'll make it real.

"Jenna, I want to make sure we are doing more than drawing boxes and lines on an org chart. I saw the blueprint we created, and it is a good start. There will be a lot of work to stitch together how the work actually flows and who the right people are to do it. I think the charter also needs to include who we should move, who we should separate, and what roles we need to go to the market to find."

Alex agreed, "Your team will be responsible for making proposals. Richard and I will be the final decision makers. I also suggest you talk to Olivia about the Move, Motivate, and Market plan as you get to that step."

"Understood," Jenna confirmed.

Tanya, the learning & development manager, still nursing her latte, spoke next, "On AI management training, I think the first hurdle is going to be the employee mindset. Too many leaders see AI as a tool that sits in the background. To confirm, our job is to teach them to see it as part of their team? If that's correct, we will need them to write clear expectations for every leader.

"We will also need to train them to provide feedback to the right people who can make the right adjustments. David mentioned you did that in your meeting the other day. Managers have a hard enough time holding real people accountable. I think my charter has to be, simply, to prepare every manager in this company to lead in a blended workforce."

Richard was impressed. "I'm not sure I would call that mandate simple. That's a big mandate, but I am glad you are up to the task."

"It has to be simple," Tanya replied. "My view is that if we get this wrong, everything else we are working on will collapse. The future org only works if leaders know how to work with AI, not against it, and the simpler we make the training, the quicker the skills are adopted."

"No, you're right. It's still a big task ahead. I'm glad you caught the vision and are ready to run with implementation," Alex interjected. "Mark, let's talk about your team for a bit."

Mark, the FP&A director, had been scribbling notes furiously. He finally looked up when Alex said his name. "Right, governance."

He paused for a moment before starting back up, "At first, I thought it was simply policy and guardrails to ensure compliance when we use AI in the process, but after digging in a bit, I think it is a lot more than that. We have to work out the element of trust with everything we are building. Our employees, customers, vendors, and everyone need to have confidence in what we have done. Our data needs to stay secure and will serve as the foundation for governance.

"I can envision building a process where a human doesn't even have to look at the data. I believe it would be reckless for us to allow that. Our task is to establish the right rules of the road. You know, what ethical standards will we uphold, what risk profile will we establish, and who will be responsible for ensuring we have the right people looking at the output at the right time."

Alex studied the three of them then turned to Mark. "Mark, you have been able to stitch all three projects together in a way that I had not thought about. Each of your charters is slightly different, but they are definitely interconnected. It's like any building project. Jenna is building the house, Tanya will teach people how to live in it, and Mark will make sure the lights stay on safely."

That got a laugh from the group and put their roles into a new light. They were in this together to build up the company in this new age of AI.

Richard looked at them, more serious now. "I want to make sure you comprehend something: you're not just project leads. You are symbolic. The rest of the organization will watch how you lead, communicate, and handle setbacks. If you show up with clarity, confidence, and humility, others will follow. If you hesitate, they will too."

Jenna raised her mug. "Then let's not hesitate."

Tanya and Mark followed, their cups clinking together in the small space between them.

Alex smiled. "Good, because from this point on, you're not just leading Talent Teams, you're showing us what this new kind of leadership looks like."

Kathy stood at the head of the small boardroom, her laptop connected to the projector. She looked around the table– seeing familiar faces, cautious expressions– and took a breath.

"Before I show you anything," she said, "let me ask a question. How many times in the last few months have we realized we were late thanking a donor?"

A few people shifted. Bill gave a small shrug.

"How often have we said, 'We should follow up with them,'

and then didn't?"

This time, a couple of quiet nods.

Kathy nodded back. "That's the gap I'm trying to solve."

She clicked to the first slide but didn't look at it.

"We've grown and have actually outgrown our current systems. We have more donors and a lot more activity, but the way we manage relationships hasn't kept pace. We're still relying on spreadsheets, manual emails, and memory; and it's starting to show. It's starting to show with everyone."

Susan was the first board member to speak up. "What are you proposing?"

"A new CRM could help us tremendously," Kathy said. "We really need something that helps us understand what's happening with our donors in real time."

Bill looked at Kathy. "We've looked at CRMs before. They're expensive, and half the features never get used."

Kathy agreed, "You're right. Most of them are just better filing cabinets. I've looked at six different systems, and the technology has come a long way."

She paused, then said, "The biggest change is the CRM's now use AI to deliver more results."

The reaction was immediate. Bill shook his head. "There it is. I was wondering when that was coming."

Susan frowned. "I don't like the idea of AI anywhere near our donor relationships."

Kathy didn't rush to defend it, but simply asked, "Can I tell you how I've been using it personally?"

That question stopped the objections in its tracks.

"I had to write a donor thank-you note a few weeks ago," she continued. "I must admit, I was stuck. I don't know, maybe it was writer's block, but I couldn't come up with a simple thank-you note. My husband had been pushing me to try AI, because I was just like you: I wanted nothing to do with it. Well, my mind was so blank that I figured it wouldn't hurt to try it out, so I did, and I was amazed at how effortlessly it gave me a starting point. Of course, I didn't just copy and paste, but it gave enough of an idea that got my creative juices flowing again."

She looked around the table. "It didn't replace me, or my voice, or my ideas. All it did was help me get past my writer's block."

Bill said, "That's different than turning it loose on our donors."

"It is," Kathy replied, "and I guarantee you, we're not turning it loose on anyone. Think of it more as an assistant and less like automation. We will have it watch for patterns that we don't have time to track. It will flag when someone hasn't given in a while, and it will suggest when to send a thank-you. The best news is that it doesn't do anything without our approval."

Susan leaned in slightly. "It would make recommendations?"

"Yes," Kathy said. "Then, we decide what to do with the information. Every message, and every outreach must and would continue to come from a real person."

Bill still wasn't convinced. "I've read enough to know these systems can go sideways. It seems to make stuff up, there are all kinds of privacy issues, and I have even heard about it having a certain bias."

Kathy agree, "All of that is true. I have seen some of the phantom answers myself. Which is why we will never leave it to its own devices."

She spoke more confidently, "We would set the rules and review the outputs. We would need to conduct the appropriate number of audits to ensure it does what we need it to. If something doesn't make sense, we stop it."

There was a pause.

"Why now?" Susan asked. "We've managed this long without it."

"Because we're starting to miss things that matter," Kathy said with a pained expression on her face. "We need more capacity if we are to do more for the kids. We're asking a small team to manage a growing network of relationships without giving them the support to do it well."

"And the new system allows you to do that?" Bill asked.

"Yes, it does. It ensures we can keep up with the growth demands placed on us. It also gives us visibility we don't have today, and it lets our team spend less time tracking information and more time actually connecting with people."

She let that sit for a moment.

"Financially," Kathy added, "it's more practical than it sounds. Hiring even one additional person to manage this would cost more than the system, and they would continue to have limited bandwidth."

Jacob, another board member, spoke from the end of the table, "Let me see if I have this right. Our assumption is that AI will help us scale to deliver the growth we are asking for, correct?"

Kathy nodded. "Exactly."

"I still don't love it," Susan stated.

"I didn't either at first," Kathy said honestly, "but the more I've used it, the more I see it differently."

The room was quiet again, but the mood had noticeably changed.

Another board member asked, "What does implementation look like?"

Kathy said, "It would be a phased rollout to ensure we could migrate all of our donors into this new tool. We would also need to deliver training for the team. I'd report back to you every quarter–what's working, what's not, and what we're adjusting."

Bill looked at Susan. She gave a small nod.

The board chair glanced around the table and asked, "Any strong objections?"

No one spoke.

"Alright," he said. "Let's move forward, with updates each quarter."

Kathy let out a breath she hadn't realized she was holding. "Thank you," she said.

As the meeting broke up, she closed her laptop slowly, with a quiet sense of accomplishment.

The sun had set by the time Richard pulled into the driveway; his mind had yet to quiet down from ruminating on the day's breakthroughs at the company. The glow of the kitchen light spilled into the evening air. Inside, Kathy was sitting at the table with a cup of tea, her laptop closed in front of her. She looked over to Richard, a soft smile on her face.

Richard hung his jacket and smiled back. "You look like you had a big day."

"And you look like someone who needs to hear about mine

before you start in on yours."

He chuckled and sat across from her. "Fair enough. How did the board presentation go?"

"Better than I expected. I walked the Board through the proposal. As expected, Bill and Susan had an 'AI is evil' pitch all worked out. Miraculously, I stayed calm, explained the plan, and reminded them that it would ultimately allow us to serve more kids. I told them this is not for technology's sake, but for the sake of the children."

"You said that? That's brilliant."

She grinned. "I did. And it worked. After some debate, they approved the proposal. Now I get to give updates at every board quarter. It's the first time I've seen them that open about innovation."

"That's huge, Kathy. I'm proud of you." He reached over and squeezed her hand. "You're modeling exactly what I've been trying to preach all day."

She tilted her head. "Sounds like your day went well, too?"

Richard told her about the executive team's progress, identifying critical roles, and top talent. Then his tone softened. "We're making progress, but it's going to be a long road. I had to have some tough conversations."

"How are you feeling about your first week back at the helm?"

"I don't know. Part of me is excited, but part of me wonders if I was ready to step back into the fray."

She laughed softly, "Well, it's too late now. Have you thought about using an AI chatbot to work through how to have some of those tough conversations? I had some help from Grantilda. She helped me frame the cost-benefit case. I even asked her how to handle skeptics. She's not perfect, but she got me unstuck when I didn't know where to start."

Richard grinned, "Look at you, leveraging your W3 teammate."

"I'm getting there," she said, taking a sip of her tea. "It's still unusual, but this could free us to do more meaningful work. The key is to do it right."

Richard thought about her words and listened to the cicadas humming in the summer night. He considered how each of them was navigating their own storms, yet they were both finding a new way forward.

"Feels like we're both learning how to lead differently," he said softly.

Kathy reached for his hand again. "Maybe that's the point."

Chapter Thirteen
Giving AI a Job

Two weeks later was a good old-fashioned roadshow where Richard and Alex could have made T-shirts about all of their stops. From the manufacturing plant to the corporate headquarters and on to a regional sales office, it reminded them of the old days; they were bringing a fresh vision. Richard really wished he could transport to each stop like one of his sci-fi books, but he knew the journey and rest were just as important for him as the time at each stop.

"Boy, this feels like déjà vu," Richard said.

Alex looked up. "You mean this trip?"

Richard shook his head. "Not exactly. I am thinking about our last big turnaround roadshow when we first brought in Olivia. I remember walking into the same rooms where people were demoralized, concerned, and we needed to get them energized by a better future."

Alex smiled. "There he is. That's the leader I remember. One that is ready to rally the troops."

Richard thought about the book on his nightstand, the sci-fi story of a starship where the AI calculated risks, predicted meteor storms, and charted courses, but never took away the captain's decision authority. That metaphor had been echoing in his mind.

Oh, how fiction sometimes mirrors real life. He had wondered if he would be in a position to share the story. Now, he decided today would be the day.

The first stop was a manufacturing plant two hours from headquarters. Richard lit up as he greeted old friends. They reminisced fondly about the early days of the company. The newer employees, who only knew him by stories, shook hands with him and couldn't help but like him.

Richard moved to the shop floor and stood in front of rows of operators wearing safety vests. The humming machinery behind him served as a metaphor in and of itself.

"You know," he began, his voice lively, "I was reading a science fiction story about a captain on a ship with a new AI system. It meant to serve the crew by answering questions faster, providing necessary information, and, in some cases, even taking control of the whole ship. At first, the crew was skeptical about this new AI system. While they used technology, this system seemed more invasive, so they were naturally resistant to it. They feared being made irrelevant, but they soon learned the benefits far outweighed any individual concerns. However, it wasn't until the ship was in critical condition that AI gave them an answer no one else had thought of, saving the whole ship.

"That's the future. We'll bring in AI to free each one of you to do your jobs better and faster. My goal is not to replace anyone. As we grow, I will need everyone on board to take advantage of that growth. That means on the manufacturing floor, AI will focus on what matters most. We will use it to make sure everyone goes home the same way they came to work. We will use it to monitor machine performance and take advantage of inputs to increase capacity."

The employees shifted in their seats, mixed emotions written on their faces. One veteran raised a hand. "Richard, I'm worried we've heard this before. Our experience is that we're next on the chopping block. I know you, Richard, but I need to hear it from you. Will you be cutting our jobs?"

Richard shook his head. "No. I'm definitely not thinking about needing fewer jobs. I expect we will need more people to handle the increased demand. My commitment to you is that everyone here will have the chance to apply their know-how to improving our manufacturing variances and OTIF. Will AI take some of the tasks off your plate? Yes, it definitely will. Which is a good thing, so you can focus on resolving problems and making the highest quality product for our customers."

Another worker muttered, "We've heard that before."

Richard said, "I am sure you have. However, you have not heard it from me. Just ask your fellow workers who were part of my team when I founded this company. They know I won't throw around false promises. I hope they will tell you that I lead differently and will listen– actually listen to you. That's what Alex and I are doing now. This roadshow is about hearing from you and being honest about where we're going."

The new employees looked at those who had worked there when Richard was CEO. All of them nodded, agreeing with everything he said. Their support sparked positive murmuring among the employees. Richard knew he had opened the door.

Richard and Alex had insisted on hosting a picnic lunch for everyone. They even manned the barbecue to grill the burgers and hot dogs themselves. He didn't want speeches anymore. He just wanted to spend time with the employees and hear what was on their minds. After he flipped his share of burgers, he moved from table to table, shaking hands, laughing at stories, and hearing what everyone was talking about.

As Richard engaged each table, the questions kept coming. Many of them weren't completely convinced, but were willing to give Richard a chance. One worker asked if the new systems would make their jobs harder at first.

"Well, change is always hard. There is a learning curve that takes time to get used to," Richard said, "but we'll make sure you get the training and support to get comfortable. If something isn't working, I want to hear about it directly. That's how we make the tools fit the people, not the other way around."

Another asked if AI would slow down production when it flagged errors. Richard smiled. "I sure hope it flags the errors. If it catches the issue early enough, it will save everyone from having to do rework later. Better yet, it will make sure it never reaches our customers. Make no mistake, we are going to have to tweak the system, and we will test it every which way from Sunday before we roll it out site-wide."

As the afternoon wound down, Richard thanked everyone who planned this day. He thanked the grill crew, the HR team, and the plant management for all of their efforts in making a great event.

After shaking a few more hands, he headed to the parking lot. As usual, Alex hit his max with people and the event long before Richard, so he wasn't surprised to see him waiting at the car with that familiar half-smile.

They took off for home and for a few moments, neither spoke. Finally, Alex cleared his throat.

"Well," Alex said, "you were always pretty good at this whole 'man of the people' thing."

Richard chuckled, "Haha. You know, as much as I love talking to people, they needed to hear straight from me that we're not cutting jobs. And they needed to see us flip a burger like anyone else, that the two of us are not above them and we're just a couple of guys who want to see this company succeed."

"No truer words were spoken. Well, maybe that's not entirely accurate," Alex said with a chuckle.

"The good news," Richard replied, "is that they believed us. They believed in what we were saying. It certainly helped to have some of the old-timers vouch for us. It would have been much harder to get them to open up without our history here. "

"Yep. We both know it'll still take time. I know Finance is way behind everyone else. Ops may be a bit further ahead, but they are cautious. The good news is that today was a win. I will take it!"

Richard nodded, watching the horizon. "One step at a time. One shift, one plant, one burger flipping lunch at a time. That's how we turn this ship."

The next day at headquarters, Richard addressed a room filled with corporate functions. Alex was there with him, providing critical leadership presence and additional insight. Emily had pulled them aside before the meeting to let them know the employees were worried about layoffs.

Richard gathered the managers in a conference room. "Look, I get it. You've seen and heard this spiel before. Just know that I will never do a spreadsheet exercise. My goal is to build capacity for every person. I believe each of you wishes you had more resources. Is that true?" Richard looked out over the room and saw heads shaking. "I am not interested in cutting people, but doing more with the resources we have. That's why we're going to invest in management training and ensure we have the AI governance structure. And yes, some of the work will change, especially the mundane, repetitive work, but that's the point: we want to give you back time for the strategic, value-added work."

Alex added, "The company implemented AI to leap over our competitors. Unfortunately, that didn't happen for several reasons. We recognize AI alone won't turn this company around. In fact, the implemented approach does the opposite. We learned a long time ago that systems don't change culture; people do."

Emily chimed in, "I have been working with Richard and Alex for a couple of months now. They have the right perspective and will do the right things to turn this company around, leveraging the AI systems we have already implemented. I am actually excited about this new direction and believe it will benefit all of us."

By the time they reached the regional sales office, the skepticism had given way to curiosity. It was clear the roadshow had beaten them to this event. The team had gathered in a hotel ballroom for an all-hands meeting. Richard walked to the center of the stage, no slides behind him, just a microphone in his hand. Richard repeated the story of the sci-fi captain and that AI would be part of the Third Workforce. He reiterated that each of them would remain at the helm.

Richard even sat down with a group of young account managers over lunch. Some seemed nervous, while a few of the driven ones were eager to sit down with the CEO. One asked, "Are we really expected to treat AI like co-workers?"

Richard laughed. "Let me ask you, if the bot helps you get ready for ten calls instead of three, who should get the credit?" He looked around at thinking faces and continued. "You do, of course. Let me ask another question. If AI spots a client problem before you notice it, who does the client thank? You. You are still the face of the relationship and will always own the client. AI becomes a way for you to serve those customers better."

By the end of lunch, laughter filled the table as they asked each other what they were going to name their bot. One of the more creative account managers said he would name it "Shurelock," because the deals would be a sure lock! Richard laughed with them and recognized that humor always helped with change management.

Over the course of the roadshow, Richard and Alex met employees in small groups, had lunches with supervisors, enjoyed coffee chats with managers, and dined with clients. They listened, answered tough questions, and repeated the same message. It was all about change management and creating space for people to share concerns.

On the last evening, Alex spoke up at a dinner with about ten mid-level managers. "Before stepping back into this role, I was doing fractional CFO work. The one thing that always surprised me was how companies could do so well even without state-of-the-art systems. When I reflect on that, I realize the companies that grew had one thing in common: the employees felt connected to each other, to the strategy, and to their leaders. That's our goal here and why we have spent the last few weeks talking with every employee."

Richard, raising his glass, said, "I'm excited about becoming the kind of company where humans and AI can work together, and where you, the crew, still steer the ship."

The room erupted in applause, even though they still had questions. They cheered because, for the first time in a long while, they believed their leaders were walking the same road with them.

While Richard and Alex were on the road, Kathy sat at her desk, laptop open, the quiet of her home office interrupted only by the ping of calendar reminders.

She had scheduled back-to-back demos with CRM vendors. Each one of them promised the world. Which Kathy knew was a global sales tactic the system would never live up to.

Kathy listened to the sales pitches about automated donor journeys, emails, reminders, and personalized outreach. A couple had the capability for predictive analytics that identified who was most likely to give again and the best times to reach out for a donation. It even provided data to know how much to ask for. Besides that, there were modules for volunteers, donor relations, and accounting integrations that made her head spin. Fortunately, she was able to leverage Grantilda to help with note-taking, so she didn't miss anything. She could focus on the conversation and ask all of her questions.

She leaned back, rubbing her temples, and said to herself, "Which one is right for us?"

That's when she decided to get Grantilda's perspective.

"Grantilda," she said, using the AI's voice capability function, "I've got three systems on the table. What is the right one for us?"

Grantilda answered her question, helping her think through the pros and cons of each vendor. It brought forth interesting nuances to consider, such as the most pressing problem she hoped to address, the value she hoped to gain, and how to approach donor engagement and retention.

"Okay, Grantilda," she said, speaking to her AI assistant, "here's my million-dollar question. Vendor A offers the best interface to simplify the internal teams' transition. But Vendor B has much better donor analytics, which will certainly make my life easier. While Vendor C is the most expensive, they offer automation and will provide the most value. I think I lean toward Vendor C, but I don't know how to justify the cost?"

Grantilda responded, "You can focus your decision on the biggest impact. Vendor C has the best embedded AI to help you scale donor engagement. It will also enable personalized outreach, automated donor journeys, and real-time tracking of every touchpoint. That means you will have a higher donor retention, substantially smarter prospecting, and ultimately raise more money for the cause, all without adding any headcount."

Kathy thought for a moment. "I see it now. While the system is more expensive, if we do this right, we can grow the business without extra headcount. This ultimately saves us money."

"That is right," Grantilda affirmed. "Position it as an investment, and pair the numbers with stories. The board will eat it up."

That afternoon, Kathy entered her CEO's office. She outlined her CRM evaluation process and shared the pros and cons matrix she had created with Grantilda's help. She also had a list of possible objections and how she would address them. Her CEO loved Kathy's approach to the project and gave her the green light to keep going.

That night, back on their porch, Richard and Kathy compared notes as they enjoyed the autumn dusk.

Richard exhaled. "It was a big day. I stood in front of hundreds of employees, some I've known for decades, others I'd never met. And no surprise, I ended up using that sci-fi story I read a few months ago, about the ship and its AI."

Kathy smiled. "So, you're Captain Kirk now?"

He chuckled, "I wish. No, they needed reassurance. They needed someone to say, 'You still matter,' and I gave them that. They're naturally cautious, given their recent treatment by management. I am so glad Alex and I did this roadshow. The employees needed to hear from their leaders instead of getting some impersonal email about the changes coming down the pike."

"Funny, I had the same kind of day as I spoke with our CEO. We talked through the plan and came up with a strategy to ensure the Board wouldn't change their minds because of the lack of trust in AI or because it's too risky."

"Sounds familiar," Richard winced.

Kathy grinned. "Fortunately, the CEO doesn't believe AI is the devil either."

Richard raised his glass in a quiet toast. "Good. I'm glad that it was a good day for you, too. We can celebrate them when they come."

"I will toast to that," she said, smiling. "Grantilda helped me frame my strategy. I am becoming a bigger fan the more that I leverage the capability."

"There she is again. Your AI teammate."

"Yeah, she's making me braver. The truth is, I'm starting to see what you've been saying all along. This Third Workforce can really help us grow without losing what makes us human."

Richard raised his glass again. "Look at us, preaching the Third Workforce from both sides of the business divide."

She chuckled, "Except my workforce is donors and yours is employees."

They sat in comfortable silence for a moment. Then Richard spoke, almost to himself, "Sometimes it feels like we're walking through fire, but maybe it's the kind of fire that makes the forest grow back stronger."

Kathy reached over and took his hand. "Then we walk through it together."

Chapter Fourteen
Making It Hold

The conference room, which doubled as a command center for the past few months, was where the Talent Team would deliver their report-out. All of the posters, workflows, and sticky notes in three colors for W1, W2, and W3 continued to adorn the walls; Olivia left them up as artifacts and reminders of the journey they were on.

Richard looked around the table at the three Talent Team leads. Jenna, Mark, and Tanya sat with a small group behind them. This was the first time many of them had been in a meeting with the CEO— naturally, a mix of eagerness and cautiousness permeated from the assembled team.

Richard began, "Alright, let's get started. You've each had time to work out your strategy for tackling the presented challenge. I am excited to see where you've landed and what direction you would like to take. Jenna, let's start with your team."

Jenna rose, clicking to a slide that showed the swim-lane diagrams they'd built. She was confident, but was still unsure how their strategy would be received.

"We've been running hard these last few weeks, and the mapping exercise has given us visibility of our whole workforce. I want to start with the good news. Some groups are way out in front, making our progress look achievable to other teams. While some groups are behind, overall, we are on track to map the organizations, identify the roles, determine who performs them, and show where AI is filling them. We have begun identifying leaders who can step in to manage the W3 workforce. I feel good where we are currently at."

Taking a deep breath, she continued, "The sales and marketing teams surprised all of us with how much AI they had already implemented. They have done a good job integrating AI into the sales funnel, including lead scoring and automated campaign adjustments. When we compared W1, W2, and W3, they had the best integration of the three. It wasn't perfect, but you could see how it was all working together. We are now working on the organizational structure and on how best to layer in AI management. The good news is that most of the team appears to be on board with the three workforce concept."

Carlos almost puffed out his chest. "I'll take that compliment, Jenna."

Jenna nodded. "You should, Carlos. Your team is a role model, but also the one that has been playing with AI the longest.

"Moving on to Operations. They're in the process of implementing predictive maintenance bots that monitor equipment health. Interestingly, they have scheduling agents working alongside planners, saving planners significant time. We're already seeing improved throughput now that the planners have adjusted their interaction with the AI agent. Well, that and restructuring to provide management a better line of sight. That said, there is still a good bit of resistance on the floor, even after your roadshow. They still expect us to cut headcount."

Richard chimed in, "Change takes time, Jenna. David needs to reinforce the idea that incorporating AI means doing more, not having less."

"Understood," Jenna replied. She then flipped to the next slide. "HR is moving along at its own pace. Julie's recruiting bot is screening candidates and scheduling interviews, freeing up recruiters to spend time sourcing and talking with candidates, which is exactly the kind of human touch AI can't replicate.

"Unfortunately, the rest of HR is behind on their roadmap for the year, which means we are behind on designing the new organizational structure. The team remains wary of the new technology. My best guess is it comes from a place of job loss fear."

Julie was silent as all eyes turned to her, but took a deep breath and said, "That is partly true. Some HR functions are further ahead, partly due to the maturity cycle. Recruiting is where many of the AI companies began their focus. We will get there, and I will continue to reinforce the benefits of this direction."

Richard decided to capture a teachable moment for all of the Talent Team leaders. "Jenna, you can't just guess at what the employees are feeling. You need to sit down with them and listen to their fears. That is a critical part of a leader's job. That goes for all three of you."

Jenna nodded, letting Richard know she would do better next time. She then moved to the next section and said, "And then there's Finance."

The slide showed a mostly empty W3 lane.

"Emily's team still handles a lot manually, including consolidations, reconciliations, and expense approvals. The quarterly close is still ninety percent driven by human effort. We found only a few basic automations, with no real AI tools reducing workload. Compared to other departments, Finance is falling behind. Which also means, very little progress on the new org design."

Before Emily could respond, Richard leaned forward with a grin and shot a look at Alex. "Well, Alex, it looks like Finance is still living in the Stone Age. What's going on, CFO emeritus? You gonna let your people get shown up by Sales?"

The room chuckled as the levity seemed to cut the tension. Alex rolled his eyes, but let the comment go. "Don't worry, Richard. Emily and I are on top of this, and we will catch up."

"It's not a criticism. Finance has the most growth potential. Imagine the efficiency once bots handle reconciliations or AI detects anomalies before they affect the books. The payoff could be significant," Jenna said.

Emily jumped in, "We know, Jenna. Now that we see how Operations and Marketing have integrated W3 into their workflows and organizations, we have a better picture of what our roadmap could look like. My team's next priority is to pilot AI in the close process this quarter."

"The bottom line from our work so far is that the groups leveraging W3 are really freeing up capacity, and we are making progress on the W3 manager identification. The data's telling us what we already suspected. When managed properly, it is a game-changing way forward, and is our top priority in the org design." Jenna set the clicker down, stepping back from the screen.

Richard nodded. "Good. Keep going, and let's make sure to come up with stories about how capacity has increased to help us combat the fear that we will still cut headcount. And Emily, I need your team to get into gear. Tanya, your turn."

Tanya stood as the participants' attention shifted from Jenna's functional maps to her.

She smiled. "Jenna's right, the gaps in Finance were obvious, but what hit us even harder was the leadership gap across the board. We realized that managers are struggling with their workloads and sense of identity. They know how to lead people. They know how to escalate IT tickets. But they've never been asked to lead both human and digital workers. That's a new skill set."

Everyone seemed to acknowledge this reality.

"We built a manager training program to help with this transition. We brought in a group of top managers to help us co-create the curriculum. We held working sessions where they shared their feedback. From there, we built training that focused on various topics like 'How do I hold an AI bot accountable if it makes a mistake? What do I say when my employee asks why the bot gets the easy work? How do I explain to my boss that the close was late because the AI didn't flag something?' These types of questions became the backbone of the training.

"We landed on a three-part structure to help every manager feel prepared to lead this new workforce. First, we ensure every manager clarifies the roles that each employee holds, both human and AI. Managers then learn how to map workflows across all three sectors and tools to write 'mini-job descriptions' for bots, just like they do for employees. Our goal is to provide a higher level of accountability and to minimize overlap of responsibilities.

"Second, managers are trained to set appropriate boundaries, build escalation paths, and initiate process review cycles for all AI tasks. If the manager is to manage the bot or the agentic agent, they need to understand what that means in practical terms.

"Finally, we teach managers how to talk about AI with their teams, including how to set the right tone so employees see AI coworkers as a source of support and job enhancement, not as competition for their jobs. We even coach them on language."

Alex chimed in and asked, "What does that sound like?"

"Instead of saying 'The bot will replace you,' we teach them to say something like 'The bot takes the busywork so you can focus on higher-value work.'"

She paused, which gave Richard an opening to ask, "In essence, you're reframing the management culture. Is that a way to look at it?"

"I guess you could put it that way, but rest assured, we have no intention of watering down the culture you are establishing. If anything, we want to strengthen it with our training."

"Good. I am excited to sit through the training for myself," Richard said, smiling.

"The first version of this program is ready, and we'll run it with twenty frontline managers next week. It will gain valuable insights, as this pilot group is a cross-section of every function. Once we have their feedback, we will make the appropriate adjustments and build a roll-out plan for the rest of the company."

Alex asked, "What if the managers push back? What if they feel like this is just one more unnecessary activity on their overflowing plate?"

Tanya replied, "We anticipated that, which is why we had our top managers help us design it. We want to ensure the training is valuable. They helped us build the case studies and various exercises to engage their peers. Quite frankly, the managers are hungry for training, especially on this topic. The last thing we want is a manager who feels stuck between people and bots, without the tools to lead both effectively. If managers can't adapt quickly, the whole W3 strategy begins to collapse. After digging into this, I am a firm believer that the Third Workforce becomes a new competitive advantage for us to augment the talented employees we have."

Richard looked at Alex to see if he had any more questions. He signaled he was good, so Richard said, "Thanks, Tanya. I appreciate how you thought through the training and roll-out plan. Please invite me to your pilot training. I will prioritize attending so I can learn with everyone else."

Tanya's eyes went wide in surprise, but she took the action item to invite Richard, and then sat down.

Mark knew he was next. He decided to stay seated as he was less comfortable standing in front of a crowd. He began by saying, "I am leading the governance team. We spent a lot of time discussing what this topic was all about. What we came up with is that governance is another layer of our culture."

He looked around the table before continuing.

"Everyone in this room has a type A, run fast personality. We saw this with the rush to implement AI into, well, everywhere. The promise of shaving an hour here or cutting headcount there was the carrot we chased after. Unfortunately, we are now experiencing the implications of speed without governance. At best, it's a gamble, a gamble with the company's future, and the odds are not in our favor, given how new these tools and systems are."

Mark opened the folder, revealing a mockup of a laminated

AI Passport	
Name and Purpose	What is this agent and why does it exist?
Owner	Who is accountable for its performance?
Data Access	What systems does it touch?
Decision Rights	What authority does it have, and where does human oversight kick in?
Guardrails	The boundaries it cannot cross.
Review Cycle	How often it gets audited and refreshed.

card titled *AI Passport*.

"Let me explain what we've been building. Every person in this company has a personnel file. Every contractor or gig worker has a contract. Yet our AI agents, the bots making decisions, moving money, and routing customer orders, have nothing. In most cases, we couldn't find a business owner. While the agent is monitoring uptime, no one is taking accountability for what they are supposed to do. That became our starting point, and it clearly needs fixing."

He held up the card. "The AI Passport is our answer. Think of it as a W3 employee file. It is basically a record for every digital worker that documents the name, purpose, owner, data it accesses, decision rights and authority it has, guardrails in place, and the standard review cycle.

Richard was intrigued. "I like this. Is this the next step after a job description?"

Mark confirmed, "Yes, employees need to understand that the same principles and accountability measures will manage the W3 workforce we hold people to. Otherwise, AI stays a tool that never gets leveraged for its full capacity."

Emily spoke up, "What does this look like in practice? Can you give me a concrete example?"

Mark smiled and flipped to the next slide, as if Emily's question was planted in advance.

"Right on cue. Let's take the demand-forecasting agent in Operations. We created its AI Passport." Mark went through the details of the passport to demonstrate what they want to deliver for all AI tools.

He continued, "That means if the bot ever goes off course, we know who's responsible, what data it touched, and we have an audit trail to know what other systems we need to audit."

Carlos jumped in, "What about our customer-facing bots? For example, our digital sales assistant is chatting with thousands of prospects. I guess we need to give it a passport, too?"

"Absolutely," Mark said. "In fact, customer-facing AI is the most critical process to have a passport. The passport defines the types of interactions it's authorized to handle and when to escalate to a human. If it goes outside those lines, the owner is accountable to step in. We don't ever want a bot to decide when a human needs to engage."

Julie had a thoughtful look on her face. "I see the benefit of this. Today, I get questions about who decides when a bot rejects a resume and when it passes it to the recruiting team. If we show that there's an owner and that the bot has clear limits, employees and candidates should feel better about how it's being managed."

"That's the point," Mark replied. "The right governance process gives us a lot more control and a comfort level that we are doing it the right way.

"Our Talent Team will issue passports for each AI agent over the next ninety days. Every function leader will be responsible for their digital workforce's passports, just as you oversee your human team's performance. We will work on building a self-sustaining process rather than a one-time compliance activity.

"In addition, we will build a map to track every transaction and build in gates that the owner has to establish before the data can move forward. This includes any financial transactions or any data that otherwise would go untouched by a human."

Richard said, with an appraising look, "Mark, I've sat through a lot of boring governance discussions in my career, but this," he gestured at the passport image, "is really creative and out-of-the-box thinking. I really appreciate your leadership on this project. I know it would have been easy to bring the same IT audit mindset, rather than come up with a completely new way to manage AI."

Alex jumped in, "I agree. I may be so bold as to say you've just rewritten what it means to have good oversight of the processes and tools we use to run the business."

Mark gave a small smile, acknowledging the compliment. "That's the only way governance works. We had to figure out how to build it into the company's SOP and underlying culture. If we treat AI as co-workers, we manage them as co-workers. It's that simple."

Richard considered all three presentations, then stood at the head of the table, pen balanced between his fingers.

"Alright," he said, "I am really pleased with the overall progress of the Talent Teams. Now, I want to hear how it feels on the ground. Are we seeing any changes in our workforce, with customers, or suppliers?"

David began, "Most manufacturing employees remain

skeptical of the technology as a way for the company to reduce headcount. On the positive side, the production planning team has turned into AI champions now that the forecasting bot is helping them spend less time chasing duplicate work and more time solving real issues."

Richard nodded. "What about cycle time? Are the activities helping at all?"

"Actually, yes. We are down eight percent, and when Finance catches up, I think we can squeeze more."

Richard smirked, glancing at Alex.

"I get it, I get it. Let's keep going," Alex responded.

Julie was next. "Managers are still generally cautious when discussing AI. Tanya's pilot can't come fast enough."

Alex asked, "Any resistance hot spots?"

"Mid-level managers who feel caught between new tools and the old metrics. I think this gets addressed during the pilot training."

Richard looked at Emily. "Emily, you are the holdout. What is your timeline to get things on track?"

Emily spoke up, "I recognize we're behind, and own up to it. We plan to pilot this quarter, and yes, Alex is hovering over my shoulder."

Alex raised his hands in mock surrender. "I prefer to call it coaching, not hovering."

Knowing it was her turn, Brianne began, "As we move to build more structure into the deployment cycle, we're implementing a simple intake process for new digital-worker requests that requires a draft passport. This will help us get it right to begin with. If a request doesn't specify the owner, data access, and appropriate guardrails, it doesn't get reviewed. I believe it will help employees navigate the change curve."

Richard looked at the Talent Teams and said, "It looks like the teams are well on their way. I will see you all next week with another review of your progress. Be sure to start gathering stories of positive progress. I want us to communicate often and broadly about the good things happening."

Chairs scraped softly as people rose. As they filed out, Richard leaned toward Alex and whispered, "Stone Age, huh?"

Alex chuckled. "Give me a chisel and a tablet bot, and I'll

write you a new story."

Richard laughed and clapped Alex on the back. He felt they were beginning to gain momentum in this turnaround.

Chapter Fifteen
Why It Still Won't Work

Richard looked around the table to make sure everyone was ready to begin. His team spread out around the outer edges of the oblong board table; he sat in the middle, Dane and Nate opposite him. This was the first official Board meeting since Richard had stepped back into the role of CEO.

He began their slide presentation once everyone was seated, "Six months have gone by fast, and I can say I am more confident than ever that we have the right strategy. The last time I led the company through a crisis, we needed to ensure we had the right people in the right roles and could execute consistently. This time, talent was only part of our strategy. I want to start by giving an overview of the processes we took the organization through. The Talent Trek 2.0 has four phases, and each one ties directly to how we run the business."

He clicked to a slide titled *Talent Trek 2.0* with the words 'Map,' 'Blueprint,' 'Governance,' and 'Training' filling four columns on the slide.

"First, we needed to understand who was doing all of the work. We mapped every process and understood who was responsible for the outcome. Second, we built a blueprint for our future organization and identified where each person and each AI bot or agent sat. The blueprint guides our investment decisions and hiring practices.

"Third, we embedded a governance model to put guardrails on every process using AI. We even created an AI passport to give the right level of visibility to the technology. Fourth, we developed and rolled out a training program for every manager to give them the tools to manage both employees and AI."

Richard looked around to make sure everyone was still with him. "We have learned that our tools, processes, and systems come and go. We know everything evolves, including organizational structure and how we run the company. What is important is how we lead, hold each other accountable, and live the corporate values. That is why we have embedded all of those disciplines into our turnaround."

He gestured toward the executive team seated around the table. "We've proven before that this company can adapt and come out stronger. I give credit to this leadership team for guiding their organization through the change. Even as we add an AI-driven workforce, we still firmly believe that leadership and culture are the real differentiators. Anyone can implement a bot into the environment; however, not many have created an ecosystem where humans and machines work seamlessly together. We found that this is our new competitive advantage, and it is paying off."

Richard then gestured to Alex. "Let's start with where we stand financially. Alex will walk us through the numbers."

Alex pulled up the next slide. A series of graphs appeared. "We are not satisfied with where we are at," Alex began, "but it's a far cry from where we were six months ago. Revenue is up six percent quarter-over-quarter. Gross margins have improved by three points. As you can see, costs are coming down, though not as fast as we'd like. Cash flow has stabilized, and for the first time in over a year, we're seeing a path forward without having to dip further into our reserves."

Nate interrupted, "Six percent is encouraging. My question is whether this is true growth or if you're just recovering what was lost. What do you see in the next six months?"

"Right now, it is mostly a recovery to our previous growth trend. As you know, we lost eleven percent last year, so we still have a gap to close. At our current trajectory, we should be back in growth mode in four months. Cost control in operations and customer engagement are our top two priorities."

Dane spoke up, "I like the recovery, but your margins are still not where we want them. What's the biggest risk to getting them back on track?"

Alex clicked to the next slide. "I figured you would ask that. Our raw materials remain volatile. This is our biggest risk to fully regaining our margins. To help offset this, David's team has introduced a lean approach to cutting waste in operations. With Julie's help, they've also focused on reducing overtime. In addition, we are working on our supply chain, renegotiating contracts to get more favorable pricing."

Dane's eyes narrowed, but he gave a slight nod. "Go on."

"Let's talk about the customer side," Richard said, gesturing to Carlos.

Carlos straightened up and said, "It's no secret that our customers have lost faith in our ability to deliver on time or with the right level of quality. We were in a doom loop of canceled meetings, delayed orders, and being pulled from their planning cycles. That shifted when we started taking ownership. Over the last quarter, we've held joint planning sessions with three of our top accounts. They're testing us with bigger orders again. It's slow going, but they're giving us chances to earn back their business. Every order we deliver on time moves us further down that road."

Nate cut in, "How can we win their business back faster? Customers are not going to wait for us to get our act together. We all know if we want growth, we have to go drive it, not wait for our internal systems to catch up completely."

Carlos looked at Nate. "There's really no shortcut, and the best strategy is to keep delivering with quality and consistency. The key to shifting their perception is to ensure that every order arrives on time, and we keep every commitment we make. There is still a good bit of goodwill towards us because of our historical relationships. Which is why they are giving us another chance."

He glanced briefly at Richard, then back to Nate. "If we keep our progress for the next two quarters, you'll see it translate into bigger contracts. Many of our customers still remember the company we used to be and are willing to give us another shot when we are ready."

"What I hear you saying is there isn't a silver bullet to get the customers back. We just have to be disciplined in our execution," Dane said.

"I think that is right. We still have good relationships with our long-term customers, so we expect to see it sooner than six months. I am cautiously optimistic right now."

Dane pushed back with one last question for Carlos, "What would prevent those same accounts from walking again if competitors undercut pricing?"

Carlos blew out a breath and said, "We have the best products, and our customers are willing to pay more for higher quality. Of course, we need to deliver on time at the promised quality levels to keep them. Once that slips, then the customers will look for cheaper products. In this business, the relationship still matters." The room went quiet for a moment before Nate nodded.

Richard spoke up, "I am also meeting with all of our current and former customers. Many of them are glad to see me back at the helm and are giving us the benefit of the doubt. This is definitely a reason they are starting to place orders with us again. Any other questions for Carlos?"

Richard waited for any last questions and said, "Okay, David, you're up."

"We've cut waste by eleven percent, and OTIF has improved by seventeen points in the last two months. Which means our targets are within sight, assuming we keep it up. Some of that came from the difficult choices of tightening schedules and renegotiating with vendors. However, the biggest driver is leveraging AI to catch breakdowns and alert maintenance before they happen. In addition, our production planners are working with better data, giving us tangible savings," David said.

Nate scribbled a note and asked, "What about supply chain costs? How are you handling the challenges with freight and other logistics? There is a lot of volatility out there right now.

"We've attacked it on three fronts. First, we are beginning to consolidate our supplier base. That will give us more leverage to negotiate better terms. Second, we're using predictive analytics to smooth out demand planning, which reduces last-minute, premium freight costs. Third, we've built a closer connection with

Finance so we can hedge where it makes sense. None of these changes erase volatility, but they give us control."

Dane had a questioning look. "Consolidating suppliers sounds like you are actually adding risk to your supply chain. One disruption of a key supplier, and you're exposed."

David agreed, "It does if you don't build contingency contracts into the model. We have primary suppliers with volume commitments, but secondary partners are pre-qualified and can step in if there's a disruption. The AI helps us monitor inventory levels and lead-time trends, so we can see problems before they become a crisis."

"Have employees given any pushback?" Nate asked.

"Sure. We had pushback early on, since no one likes the idea of a bot doing their job better than they can. All it took was a near-miss catch by the system that avoided a two-day line stoppage to change their minds. Most employees now see the value, and AI has become a co-worker they rely on."

Richard interjected, "That's been one of the success stories. Once employees saw the system helping their performance instead of taking their jobs, the culture began to shift."

The updates rolled on, each executive taking their turn at the table. Emily walked the group through Finance's progress utilizing AI. Dane pressed her on cash flow stability and debt covenants, but Emily adeptly answered his barrage of questions. She topped it off by showing their month-over-month improvements and explaining how she was keeping the company liquid.

Julie followed up with HR. She outlined the early signs of improved engagement scores, noting that managers and employees were responding positively to the training. Nate asked whether the gains would be sustainable when the next wave of AI integrations began. Julie paused and shared that all the changes were becoming part of the culture and the way they worked, but it would take time for it to become part of the company's ethos.

Finally, it was Brianne's turn to give an update on the current AI roadmap. She went through a variety of projects and recent implementations. "We've focused more energy on change management, and have begun to figure out what is next on the AI horizon that would benefit us."

"How do you do that without chasing every innovation?"

Nate questioned.

Brianne smiled. "By asking ourselves three questions about any new technology. Does this tool align with our strategy? Will it augment our current activities? And will it strengthen the human side of the workforce rather than weaken it? If it doesn't pass all three, it doesn't move forward."

Dane glanced at Richard. "I like the discipline you put around AI. How do you keep up with it when the tech moves faster than you can run a pilot test?"

Brianne didn't hesitate, "We build a flexible architecture and every AI tool we deploy now gets an AI passport, and an owner. That means we can swap in new tools without breaking the system. We're not betting everything on one model. We have built an almost plug-and-play framework. That's how we stay in front."

Richard watched her field the questions with a sense of pride. This was the same Brianne who, months earlier, had been only about implementing the new tech. Now, she was defending the company's three workforce strategy in front of an extremely tough room.

"This is the picture I wanted you to see," Richard said. "While our numbers are progressing nicely, the evidence of leadership, culture, and accountability fundamentals is the key reason we are winning again."

Dane and Nate were pleasantly surprised by what they had heard and seen, and it showed on their faces.

"The numbers certainly show progress, and your stories do suggest the change is real. If you keep proving it quarter over quarter, then maybe you'll convince us that this company can be more than just a recovery story," Dane said.

Richard allowed himself a faint smile. "That's exactly what we intend to show you."

The formal board meeting wrapped up with polite handshakes and quiet side conversations. One by one, the executives gathered their papers and left the room. It was time to move into the private session of the board.

When the door clicked shut behind the last of the executive team, what had been structured and polished became direct and unvarnished, leaving only four men at the long table looking at each other, as if asking, "Who goes first?"

Dane began, eyes on Richard, "All right. Now that it's just us, tell me straight. How's the team really doing? Are they capable of delivering what you've promised?"

Richard took a moment, glancing toward Alex before answering, "They're not perfect, but they're committed. Even Emily, who was the slowest to come around, is now pushing her team to use AI tools in Finance. Julie has stabilized HR and brought energy back into leadership training. Carlos is rebuilding customer confidence. David's operations team is showing results, as expected. Brianne has governance under control and has shifted to a strategic thought partner. I believe they're all on board. They understand what's at stake and they're ready to deliver."

Nate folded his arms, unconvinced. "No weak links?"

Richard shook his head. "They all have their learning curves, but they're aligned, and alignment is half the battle."

Turning toward Alex, Dane asked, "What else do we need to finish the job?"

Alex began, "Two things. First, we should think about refinancing. The current debt load is manageable, but if interest rates go any higher, we will begin to feel a cash pinch.

"Second, skills. There are still gaps, especially in analytics and digital operations. We're working on that through our strategic workforce planning, creating a Move, Motivate, Market plan to redeploy talent, close gaps, and acquire capabilities we don't have yet; however, it's a work in progress."

Richard added quietly, "Mainly, we just need time."

Nate was silent for a long moment. He tapped his pen on the table before looking at Dane. Dane gave a small nod, and Nate leaned forward.

"There's another conversation we need to have," Nate said. "About the exit."

Richard's eyes narrowed slightly. "Exit?"

"Yes. We are in year four of the hold. Our investors are expecting us to turn this around and get out. We've been modeling scenarios, but one way or another, we'll need to move within the next year."

Alex asked, "Isn't that a bit fast?"

Dane confirmed, "We have momentum on our side, but

windows close quickly in this business. The question is which door we walk through, and when."

The silence persisted. Richard leaned forward and said, "If we're discussing exit, then let's be serious. What are the real options available?"

Nate replied, "There are three options on the table. We can sell to another PE firm, sell to a strategic buyer, or take the company public."

"All of them are predicated on you delivering a trailing twelve months EBITDA growth," Dane added.

Richard asked, "What are you guys thinking?"

Dane interjected, "If we can buy a year, build another layer of capability, and continue closing the skills gap, an IPO becomes realistic, which would be my preference."

Richard then said, "You know, we stepped back in because we wanted to rebuild the company we care about. I recommend a path that maintains value for everyone: shareholders, employees, and customers. I would hate to be back in the same place after we've worked so hard to rebuild the culture and the brand."

"Endurance is a noble goal, Richard, but don't lose sight of reality. We're investors. We don't have the luxury of endless patience or time," Dane said.

Richard looked him in the eyes. "And I'm a builder. My job is to ensure that what we're selling has more than just short-term appeal. With more time, we can deliver something worth buying, and worth keeping."

Nate finally spoke, "Get your EBITDA up and give us two more quarters of growth, and we'll revisit which door makes the most sense."

Richard said, "That is fair enough. I will keep this on the next agenda to see where we are at."

Richard sat down in the corner booth for their weekly date night and asked Kathy, "How about you? How's the CRM project?"

"It's finally turning a corner. At first, the team resisted…a lot; they didn't want a new system. You know what I'm talking about," she said, laughing. "They were convinced the old system was great, and they didn't need any additional functionality. It's no different from the doubts you've described from your operations team. Instead of forcing it, I framed it the way you've been talking about it, as part of the workforce."

Richard smiled.

"Also, I gave the system a passport, just like you did. I made sure to shift the conversation to that of onboarding a new teammate. I was actually surprised by how helpful that language would be when implementing AI. Since we moved it out of being an IT project, people were more inclined to give it a fair shot."

Kathy's voice became more animated, "And when the first pilots went live, the results were obvious. Reports that used to take three hours finished in three minutes. The skepticism is fading, but we still have some work to do. Though George did ask the staff, 'What else can it do?'"

The waiter brought their drinks. Richard said, "Thanks," and turned back to Kathy.

"The best moment," Kathy continued, pausing as if to savor it, "was when one of my most vocal skeptics, someone who had resisted this initiative from the get-go, came into my office and said, 'I must admit, I was wrong about your system. It just gave me back two hours a day.' That was the breakthrough."

She raised her glass halfway to her mouth, "My board is thrilled. We have the green light to roll out company-wide next month, and this time, people are excited. They're not dragging their feet anymore."

Richard chuckled, shaking his head. "Sounds like you've been running your own version of the Third Workforce playbook."

"Maybe," she said with a playful smile, "but it works."

Chapter Sixteen
What Leadership Looks Like Now

The coolness of early spring hung in the air as Richard and Alex stepped out of the cab and into the sleek glass lobby of the private equity firm's headquarters.

For months, they had fought to prove the turnaround wasn't a mirage. The situation was completely different from the last time they'd walked these halls. Questions loomed from the owners and investors about whether the company could recover. They knew it was a Hail Mary to bring the two founders back to their roles. Today felt like a complete one-eighty from that day. Today, they came with a year of results behind them and the prospect of a much brighter future ahead.

As they rode the elevator up, Alex chuckled out loud, "I just remembered you called me a CFO in the Stone Ages. Do you remember that?"

Richard smirked. "Finance was still chiseling numbers on stone tablets. You have to admit, the team was way behind everyone else."

Alex shook his head. "You're not wrong. It's amazing how much can change in six months. I am still amazed that Emily is able to close the books in three days instead of nine because of the AI tools. The audit team called last week and said our documentation was the cleanest they've seen in ages."

They got off the elevator and were escorted to the familiar boardroom. Nate and Dane were already waiting.

"Gentlemen," Nate said, standing to shake their hands. "It's good to see you again. Thanks for making the trip."

Dane started the discussion, "Let's get started, shall we? I read through the Board deck, and I am even more surprised by the speed at which you have not only recovered but also accelerated growth. It seems we made the right move by bringing the two of you back in. Because of your success, I'm eager to discuss what the future looks like."

"The story is pretty simple," Richard said. "Employee engagement is up. Customers are re-engaging. We've now delivered eight straight months of growth. Revenue is climbing, margins are stronger, and the pro forma value of this company has surged; so yes, I too am anxious about talking expansion."

Alex jumped in, "I think we're surprised, as well. We know having the right leaders makes a world of difference, and that's why you brought us back in the first place. That said, revenue is up twelve percent year-to-date. Our margins improved by three hundred basis points, OTIF is holding above target for the third month in a row, and cash flow is as healthy as it's been in years. The turnaround is clearly showing on the balance sheet."

Nate replied, "Twelve percent is better than we expected. It's great for organic growth. Are you pulling any levers that won't be sustainable?"

"No. Everything we are doing is structural and completely sustainable. What is most exciting is that our customers are returning with more confidence than ever. This is fueling the growth in organic orders. At the same time, efficiency gains from AI are reducing costs and freeing capacity."

"That's what we wanted to hear," Dane said, "which is why we want to look beyond just organic growth. Where do we take this company next?" He slid a folder forward.

"We want you to expand geographically. Which of the three markets– Europe, South America, or Asia– do you prefer? Each offers scale, but each comes with risk."

Richard studied the pages. "Alex and I have talked about

international expansion. Each region has its pros and cons. Whatever we do, we will need to build out a global team. I think the question back to you is, do you want the easy but expensive play in Europe, the risky but lucrative play in South America, or a huge and much more complex opportunity in Asia?"

Nate interjected, "Can your team handle M&A without losing focus on domestic growth?"

Richard considered the question. "No matter which way we go, I will need to keep the team focused on the right priorities. We would likely need to carve out a small team to handle integration so we don't defocus everyone else on driving growth at home."

Alex added, "From a financial perspective, the markets have different growth potential. Europe may be easier to enter, but it will offer us less upside due to the higher cost. South America and Asia are definitely cheaper and could be a nice uptick in our profits. However, Asia would require the most capital to capture the market. It could have the most upside with that investment."

Dane looked at them thoughtfully. "Do you have a preference? It sounds like you've already thought about it. Where did you land?"

Richard paused, then spoke carefully, "Every time we talk about global expansion, we land on South America. It fits our DNA; it's fast-growing, and it gives us a chance to prove our model travels; it's also in our time zone, so in many ways, it's easier to manage; however, we'd need to prepare for volatility, both politically and economically– that's the trade-off. In our opinion, South America is the one worth pursuing."

Nate pressed, "How is the capability of your leadership team to expand globally?"

"After the change from the last twelve months, I think they are ready to step things up to the next level. If we give them the resources, I think they will do just fine."

Alex didn't look convinced and added with hesitation, "To afford an expansion into new geographies, the balance sheet would need to be cleaned up. We would then need to restructure the debt to free up capital. The fastest way to enter the market is through acquisition. I don't think we should try going in from scratch."

"Clearly, you have thought about this strategy if you're already thinking about the debt structure?" Nate asked.

Alex shrugged. "We need to refinance within the next quarter, and it has me thinking about what's next. Refinancing gives us room for expansion or to pursue a deal without unnecessarily straining operations. I understand you're comfortable with an over-leveraged company if it is growing, but my preference would be to make sure we have a good balance and not put the company in jeopardy."

The room went quiet for a beat. Nate spoke up again, "I think we should go to South America. You're right, Europe is too safe, and Asia would be a big undertaking. I want to expand, but I am not willing to risk all of the gains we've made this year."

Richard looked at Alex, then back to the two investors. "We are on board with going fast into South America. Give us a month, and we will come back with our strategy and potential acquisition targets."

Dane shifted in his seat. "Great, I'll have my assistant make the meeting. We've talked about organic growth and the potential of global expansion. We know both of those plays take time, and time is the one thing we don't have in abundance. We are already in the fourth year of the hold, so we've been evaluating domestic companies that could help us move faster."

Richard's eyebrows shot up.

Continuing, Nate brought up a younger competitor that was smaller but very aggressive in their industry. Not a direct competitor, but one that could expand their portfolio.

"This company has been punching above its weight, and its culture isn't far from yours. They are entrepreneurial, fast-moving, and have been able to take a lot of market share in a short amount of time," Nate said.

Alex was surprised. "And you think we should buy them?"

"We think you should seriously consider it. They'd give you immediate international presence, more capacity, and credibility in markets you'd take years to build on your own. They would also double your customer base overnight," Dane said.

Richard shook his head, "They're already making inroads into Europe. Doesn't that fly in the face of our last discussion about global expansion?"

"You could let them continue into Europe, and then you go buy another company in South America," Nate said. "All of a sudden, you're global, not just international."

Alex crossed his arms. This was moving quickly in a direction he wasn't comfortable with financially. "I would definitely want to do due diligence. My main concern is integration, which can be very messy. Culture integration is the most important part of the equation. I've seen companies with great cultures buy someone who then poisons the well. If we don't do this right, we risk losing the very trust we've worked to rebuild, and before you say anything, I know we are looking to buy a company in South America. The difference is that we would buy a local company, which would naturally have a different culture."

Dane said, "True, but remember, the kind of scale we are talking about will attract investors. You've proven you can turn this ship around. Now you need to prove you can grow it into something much bigger."

Richard took a deep breath. The thought of adding another workforce, and yet a third culture, not to mention the complexity that comes with all of it, was both exciting and terrifying. "If we go down this path," he said, "I want to really make sure culture lines up. We have just spent a ton of energy and time building our current culture. I would hate to see top talent leave because we can't keep it consistent."

Nate agreed, "That's exactly why we're putting this one in front of you. We want the two of you to dive in and do your own due diligence."

Alex let out a dry chuckle. "Well, at least it isn't boring anymore."

"Welcome to the PE world. We have our direction: keep the momentum going and continue to deliver growth. Alex, you will work with our team to refinance the balance sheet, so we have room to make these moves. Let's connect after you've had time to look at acquisition targets in South America. We will get you read into due diligence for this new acquisition. That's when you will be able to look under the hood for culture."

Nate added, "You've proven yourselves to us. If you bring us a robust plan with the timelines, your leadership needs, and the financial impacts, we'll move quickly."

Richard nodded. "We are clear on the next step. Give us a few weeks, and we'll get back to you about South America."

When Richard and Alex stepped out of the glass building, they paused and looked at each other. Neither spoke; however, both of them were thinking the same thing. They knew the world of PE-backed companies would always result in a sale or some form of event. They just hadn't anticipated that the conversation would happen so quickly.

Alex cleared his throat and said, "I'll be honest, Richard, this is all really exciting. When we took over again and started talking about the Third Workforce, I thought we would be out in six months. Everything we did, from treating AI as an employee to giving it a passport, seemed pretty strange. Now look at us."

Richard laughed. "Since we're being honest, I thought Olivia was off her rocker. You're right, look at us. We are at the forefront of changing how managers lead and how employees interact with this new technology. Did you hear one of the teams is actually coaching the bots like they're new hires?"

Alex shook his head, laughing, "No, who would have thought?"

Richard smiled back. "Olivia did. She saw it before any of us. You realize, we will need to get her back as we start buying these companies. We'll need her help for integration and assessing the cultural fitness of these companies."

"Yes, great thinking. Every breakthrough we've had traces back to her ability to translate the abstract into something people can actually work with. We may have to smooth Julie's feathers, though. I think she will see this as competition now."

They started walking to their hotel. Richard replied, "You're probably right. We can tell her that it is not a sign of our confidence in her abilities; we are just going to need all of the help we can get to pull this off."

"Here's to the beginning of something new."

Richard glanced up at the skyline. For the first time in a year, he could feel the excitement of starting a new trek. They were now charting a future no one had fully imagined. "To something new."

Epilogue
The Work Ahead

The studio lights blinded Richard as he adjusted his tie. Across from him sat the host of one of the country's top business shows. The cameras were rolling, and a national audience was waiting to hear from the business turnaround expert.

The producer signaled. The red light blinked. They were live.

"Welcome back," the host began. "Today, we're joined by Richard Curtis, the CEO who helped lead his company through one of the most significant transformations of the modern era, blending human, digital, and external workforces into what many now call the Third Workforce. Richard, thank you for joining us."

Richard smiled, his voice steady but warm, "Thank you for having me."

The host looked over and asked, "Richard, the headlines have called your story everything from a turnaround miracle to the blueprint for the workforce of the future. However, I'd like to start with something I read in an old article. A year ago, you told a team that this all began with a, what, science fiction story?"

Richard chuckled, the memory coming back. "I haven't thought about that in a while. It's funny, because I was sitting in my office reading a sci-fi book when I got the call from my old partner, Alex Washington, to rejoin the company we founded. That story became a foundation for the story I used to sell the workforce on the value of AI. I let them know that one day we would all be working alongside technology, like some of the big sci-fi TV and movie franchises. That image stuck, as everyone had seen Star Wars or Star Trek at some point in their lives. I just flipped the question to them. What if we treated AI as coworkers? That idea, half a joke at the time, became the foundation for everything we did."

The host then asked. "And now, it's a year later. You completed a turnaround and have acquired a couple of companies to aggressively expand into Europe and Latin America. All this after fully embracing your three workforce model. The growth trajectory is impressive."

Richard exhaled, "It certainly has been an action-packed eighteen months." He went on to share their story of following the Talent Trek 2.0, training managers, rebuilding customer confidence, which all allowed them to capture the growth.

"Richard, what caught a lot of attention lately was your risk of expanding into a tangential market and pushing into Latin America, at the same time. That sounds like a lot of change beyond what we already spoke about."

Richard agreed and said, "When we looked at what we needed to accelerate our growth, going international was one of the most obvious choices. We had a strong domestic recovery, but the real opportunity lay in serving customers who wanted us closer to their markets. That was why we decided to acquire a local competitor to expand our operations into Latin America, leveraging local supply chains, and serving our customers more quickly. It gave us credibility with our global accounts that had all but written us off years ago.

"Now, we're seeing the same momentum in Europe, especially since our recent acquisition, which already had a decent presence there. We have been thoughtful and taken more than a few risks, but step by step, we're becoming a global platform, not just a domestic player."

The host nodded, then pivoted, "You mentioned your recent acquisition, which surprised some people. Why was that move so important?"

Richard allowed himself a small smile. "The company we

acquired had a good culture fit with ours. I fought to dive into the details of the culture, as I knew that could be the single biggest issue with integrations. Oh, and they also moved at our pace, so speed was not going to be an issue. They gave us a European presence overnight and brought capabilities from an adjacent industry that complemented our own. We served many of the same customers, so it made sense. I will be the first to say that integration is never easy, but our teams have worked shoulder-to-shoulder to make it work, and so far it has proven to be a great strategy."

"Should we expect more deals? What's next on the M&A front?"

Richard gave a knowing glance and shook his head slightly. "You know I can't comment on specific opportunities. What I can say is that we'll continue to evaluate inorganic growth in the same way we looked at the recent ones. We will only buy someone when they align with our vision and our culture. I am not about to sacrifice the company just to be bigger."

The host didn't press as he knew he wasn't going to get anything from Richard.

"You've gone from near-collapse to being a shining star. Is an IPO in the future for you?"

Richard paused. The camera lights softened in his mind, replaced by flashes of memory, the messy boardroom debates; Tanya's first training pilot; Mark's firm hand on governance; Julie's Move, Motivate, Market plan; Alex's jokes about chisels in Finance. And Kathy, steady as ever, reminding him that leadership wasn't just about business, but about people.

"I don't know exactly what's next," he admitted. "I would never have expected to return to the company I founded and sold to lead a turnaround. So, when you ask what's next, your guess is as good as mine—a sale to another PE or maybe an IPO. Time will tell. I'm very proud of the team and excited to see how far we can take this. No matter what's next…" Richard smiled, eyes gleaming. "It's been one heck of a ride."

"Richard, thank you, and congratulations on showing the world what leadership in the Third Workforce looks like."

As the cameras faded to black and the crew started to move, Richard sat quietly for a moment. He wasn't thinking about the spotlight or the company's EBITDA. He was thinking about the story that had started it all, a science-fiction warning that became a blueprint for reality.

He knew their story wasn't finished.

Later that evening, the studio lights were gone, replaced by the warm glow of the lamp in Richard and Kathy's living room. The rerun of the live coverage was still playing silently in the background, with stock tickers scrolling across the bottom of the screen.

Kathy handed him a glass of wine and sat beside him. "You did well today," she said.

Richard chuckled. "I didn't trip over my words, at least."

She gave him the look that meant she wasn't going to let him deflect. "You've come a long way, Richard. The company, the people, even you. The question they asked at the end... It's not going away. What's next?"

Staring at the muted TV, he said, "That's the thing. We've climbed this mountain. We've rebuilt the culture, restored the growth trajectory, and expanded globally. Something no one thought possible. As much as I have enjoyed proving to myself that I can still do it, part of me wonders if it's time to step back."

Kathy sipped her wine. "Only part? What is the other part of you saying?"

He smiled faintly. "The other part thinks the real adventure hasn't even started. The Third Workforce is still evolving. There are new international frontiers to explore. Asia is still out there, and the question of IPO is a valid one. Someone's going to need to lead the company through this next part of the journey."

She set her glass down. "With all of the uncertainties, there is one thing I know. Whatever we decide to do, we will do it together."

Richard reached for her hand, squeezing it gently. "You're right. Whatever's next, we'll figure it out the same way we always have."

For a moment, they sat in silence, the muted TV flickering in the background. Richard glanced at Kathy and smiled. The story wasn't finished. Not by a long shot.

Appendix

Return on Relationship Diagram

Skills

Systems

RoR

Social Connection

Talent Trek 2.0 Roadmap

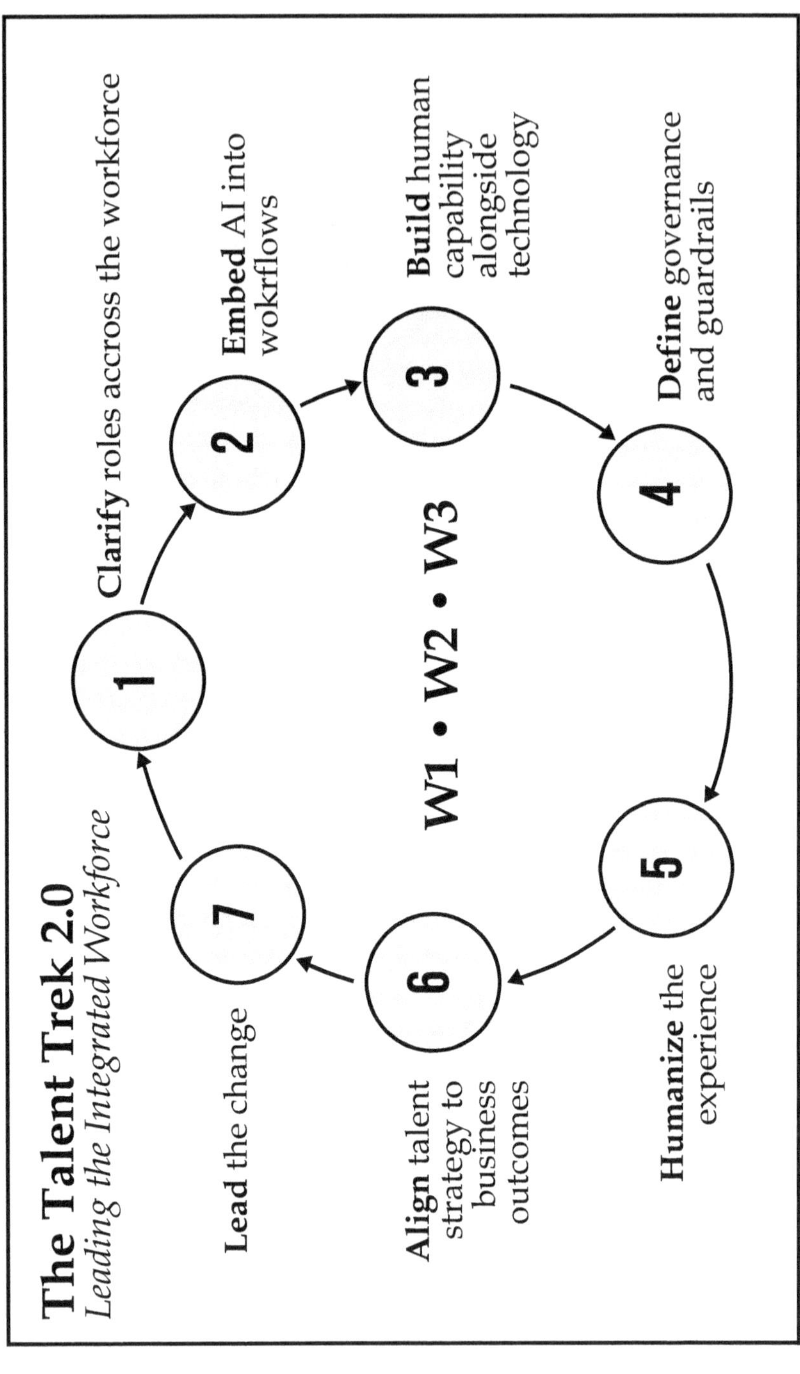

9-Box Grid for Talent Review

4 New to Role	**2** High Potential	**1** Proven Star
7 Inconsistent	**5** Core Employee	**3** High Performer
9 Action Required	**8** Contributor	**6** Pro in Position

Potential

Performance

Relational Role Mapping Worksheet

Relational Role Mapping

Identify key relational roles within your function. These roles often go unrecognized in job descriptions but are critical to how work actually gets done. Use this worksheet to identify individuals who currently play, or need to play, each role accross your workforce (W1, W2, W3).

Connector
Bridges accross teams or functions to ensure flow of information.

Signal Amplifier
Spreads urgency, insight, or strategy accross the organization.

Bridge
Ensures continuity accross W1 (Employees), W2 (External Talent), and W3 (AI/Automation).

AI Passport

Name and Purpose	What is this agent and why does it exist?
Owner	Who is accountable for its performance?
Data Access	What systems does it touch?
Decision Rights	What authority does it have, and where does human oversight kick in?
Guardrails	The boundaries it cannot cross.
Review Cycle	How often it gets audited and refreshed.

AI Passport

Name and Purpose	
Owner	
Data Access	
Decision Rights	
Guardrails	
Review Cycle	

CREATIVE® Leadership

Communication

Resilience

Empowerment

Adaptability

Team Building

Integrity

Vision

Emotional Intelligence

The CREATIVE Leadership model is trademark of Evolve HR Solutions

Acknowledgments

Writing a second book in a series is different from writing the first. While there is comfort in returning to familiar characters, putting them into a situation new to everyone was a challenge. I felt the weight of the responsibility to write this one because those who read the first one already have a baseline of expectations. Leading the Third Workforce challenged me in ways I did not expect, and several people helped make this book possible.

First, I want to thank Bill Chinn for always encouraging me in my business and my writing. Your friendship, support, and belief in this work meant more than you probably realize.

To my wife, Mollie Lupinacci, thank you for supporting all of my crazy ideas over the years. Writing, speaking, teaching, building businesses, and chasing adventure around the world only work because of the patience, encouragement, and stability you provide behind the scenes. I could not do any of this without you.

To Jennifer Welch, thank you for the incredible support throughout this project. Your editing, design work, and desire to create the next great American novel pushed me to a level of professionalism with these ideas in ways I deeply appreciate.

I also want to thank Jeremy Lupinacci for helping to

solidify many of the ideas behind the Third Workforce and, more importantly, for helping to capture and record them before they disappeared into one of my many notebooks or LinkedIn posts.

And finally, thank you to Nathan Neufeld and Carlos Chaves for continuing to cheer me on and encourage me to write the follow-up to The Talent Advantage. Sometimes all a writer needs is a few good people reminding him that the work matters.

This book may have my name on the cover, but it was shaped by many conversations, challenges, debates, and relationships along the way. Thank you for being part of the journey.

– Jeff Lupinacci

About the Author

Jeff Lupinacci has worked with leaders and organizations for more than three decades to align business strategy with talent. He is known for identifying the right leaders for critical moments—and for helping them step into roles where they can perform at their highest level. Along the way, he has led global talent functions for complex, growth-oriented companies, shaping how they hire, develop, and integrate performance-driving talent.

He is the founder of Evolve HR Solutions, where he advises executive teams and private equity–backed businesses on leadership, workforce strategy, and the challenge of building organizations ready for what comes next. His work centers on placing top-tier talent while helping leaders rethink how work is designed and how their businesses operate.

Jeff is the author of *The Talent Advantage*, an Amazon best-selling business novel on the role of talent in driving growth; the host of *The Leadership Puzzle* podcast, where he explores how leaders navigate complexity in real time; and an adjunct professor at Baylor University, teaching in the Executive MBA Program. He lives in Texas with his wife and their two doodles.

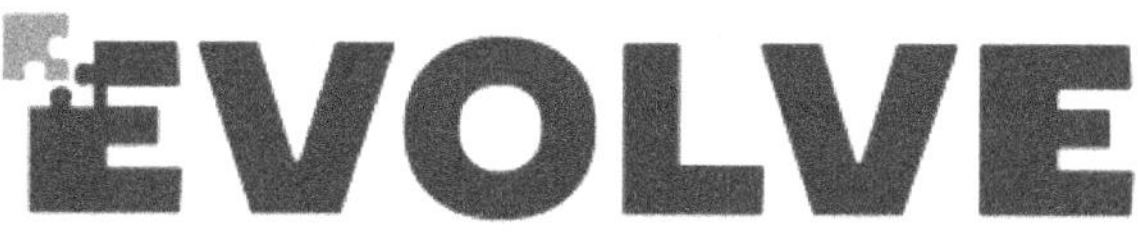

HR SOLUTIONS

We believe the future of business will be shaped by how effectively organizations integrate people, technology, and capability into a unified workforce strategy. As work continues to evolve, organizations must rethink not only who performs the work, but how work gets done, how leaders operate, and how culture scales in increasingly complex environments.

Our approach focuses on talent, leadership development, and workforce transformation. We partner with organizations to help them identify the right leaders, strengthen leadership capability, and build workforce strategies designed for long-term growth.

Executive Search

We specialize in identifying top talent who are at the intersection of capability and your organization's culture. Our core expertise centers on strategic leadership roles in manufacturing organizations. This allows us to bring transformative talent from Operations, including Supply Chain and Procurement, as well as the corporate functions like HR, Commercial Leadership, and Finance.

Leadership Development

We build flexible development programs that help leaders strengthen their communication, build accountability, improve decision-making, and strategic thinking. We blend practical application, coaching, and real business discussion to create personal growth that leaders can immediately apply back into the organization.

The Third Workforce & Workforce Transformation

We help organizations think strategically about workforce integration, governance, leadership readiness, and building organizations where people and technology work together effectively.

Learn more: www.evolvehrs.com
Connect: hello@evolvehrs.com

The Leadership Puzzle

Podcast

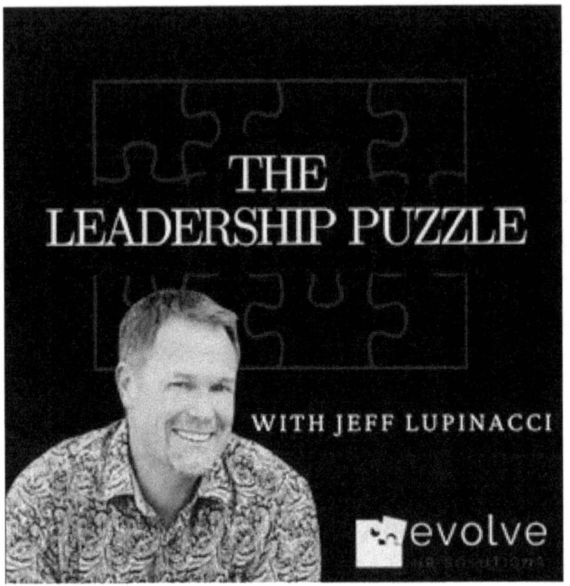

Hosted by Jeff Lupinacci, *The Leadership Puzzle* brings together conversations with executives, entrepreneurs, authors, athletes, military leaders, HR executives, and business operators to talk honestly about leadership, growth, decision-making, resilience, culture, talent, and the realities of leading people through change.

The conversations are practical, thoughtful, and grounded in real experience — not leadership clichés or buzzwords.

Topics often include:

- Building strong leadership teams
- Navigating organizational change
- Talent and workforce strategy
- Emotional intelligence and resilience
- Leadership mistakes and lessons learned
- The future of work and AI
- Accountability, culture, and execution
- What leadership actually looks like behind the scenes

At its core, *The Leadership Puzzle* is about helping leaders think differently, learn from others, and continue growing as the demands of leadership continue to evolve.

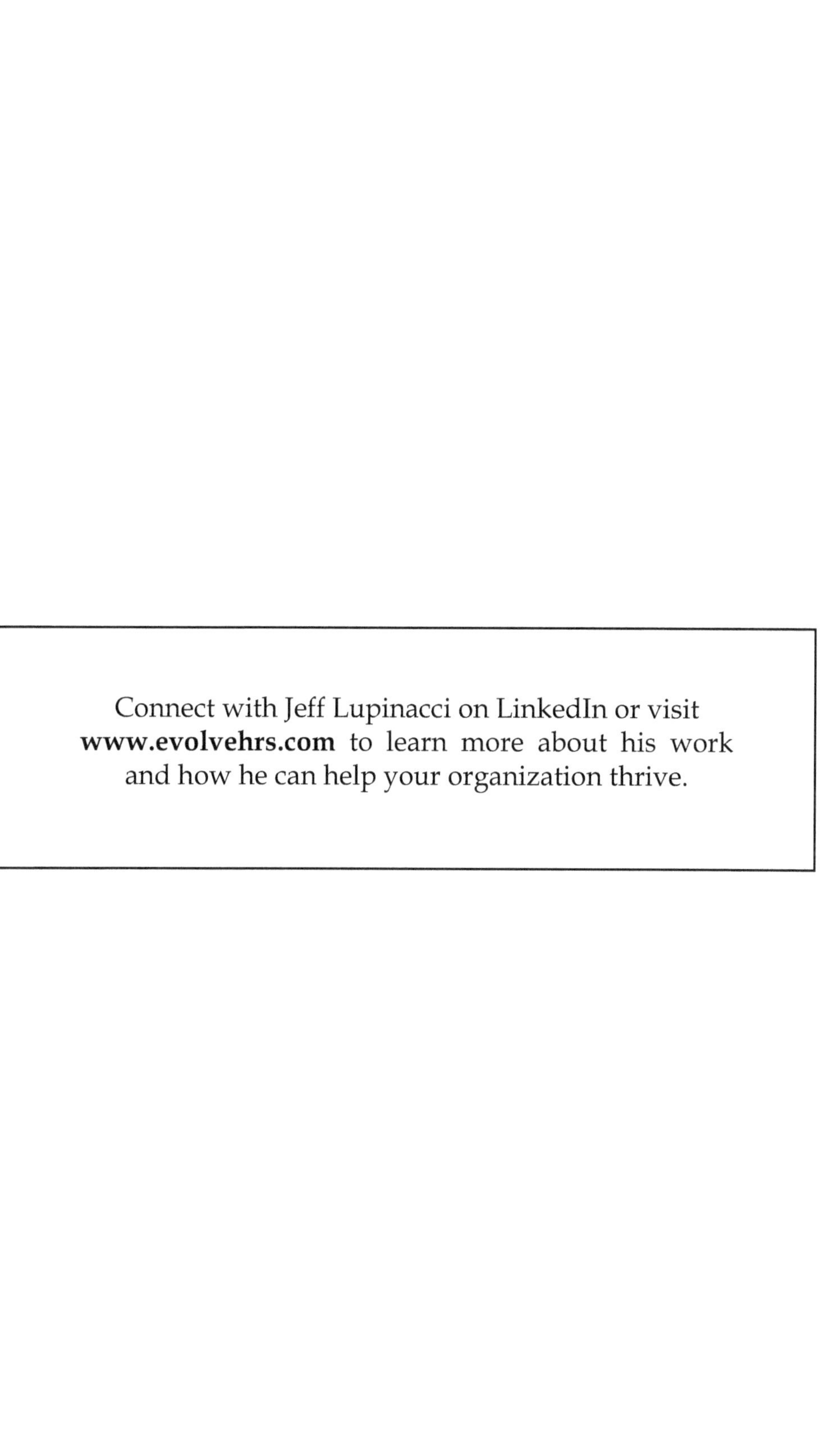

Connect with Jeff Lupinacci on LinkedIn or visit **www.evolvehrs.com** to learn more about his work and how he can help your organization thrive.

www.ingramcontent.com/pod-product-compliance
Lightning Source LLC
LaVergne TN
LVHW010658110826
845149LV00014B/3147
* 9 7 9 8 9 9 0 5 4 7 8 3 4 *